Collins

11+
Non-Verbal Reasoning

Practice Papers
Book 3

Beatrix Woodhead, Trinity Francis
and Piers Knight

Introduction

The 11+ tests

In most cases, the 11+ selection tests are set by GL Assessment, CEM or the individual school. You should be able to find out which tests your child will be taking on the website of the school they are applying to or from the local authority.

These single subject practice test papers are designed to reflect the style of GL Assessment tests, but provide useful practice and preparation for all 11+ tests and common entrance exams.

The score achieved on these test papers is no guarantee that your child will achieve a score of the same standard on the formal tests. Other factors, such as the standard of responses from all pupils who took the test, will determine their success in the formal examination.

Collins also publishes practice test papers, in partnership with The 11 Plus Tutoring Academy, to support preparation for the CEM tests.

Contents

This book contains:
- four practice papers – Tests A, B, C and D
- a multiple-choice answer sheet for each test
- a complete set of answers, including explanations.

Further multiple-choice answer sheets can be downloaded from our website so that you can reuse these papers: collins.co.uk/11plus

Non-verbal reasoning

Non-verbal reasoning assesses a child's ability to see patterns and relationships independent of language. The questions feature shapes, pictures and patterns and allow children to demonstrate their ability to analyse, deduce and infer from close observation.

Non-verbal reasoning tests provide schools with an indication of a child's potential to work successfully with abstract concepts. The results are good indicators of future learning and success in a number of subject areas.

It is particularly important to provide non-verbal reasoning practice as your child may not have come across this type of question before.

Getting ready for the tests

Spend some time talking with your child before they take the tests, so that they understand the purpose of the practice papers and how doing them will help them to prepare for the actual exam.

Agree with your child a good time to take the practice papers. This should be when they are fresh and alert. You also need to find a good place to work, a place that is comfortable and free from distractions. Being able to see a clock is helpful as they learn how to pace themselves.

Explain how they may find some parts easy and others more challenging, but that they need to have a go at every question. If they 'get stuck' on a question, they should just mark it with an asterisk and carry on.

At the end of the paper, they may have time to go back and try again.

Multiple-choice tests

For this style of test, the answers are recorded on a separate answer sheet and not in the book. This answer sheet will often be marked by a computer in the actual exam, so it is important that it is used correctly. Answers should be indicated by drawing a clear pencil line through the appropriate box and there should be no other marks. If your child indicates one answer and then wants to change their response, the first mark must be fully rubbed out. Practising with an answer sheet now will reduce the chance of your child getting anxious or confused during the actual test.

The test questions

Each test is made up of five sections, with instructions, an example and some practice questions at the beginning of each section, followed by 12 questions. In the actual exam, each section would be administered and timed separately, with the invigilator reading out the instructions, checking the practice questions and then timing the section. For the purposes of practising, however, the papers can be used in different ways, and three options are set out below.

OPTION 1: Read through the instructions with your child. Get them to complete the practice questions and check the answer key, then allow six minutes for the 12 test questions. If they have not finished in the time, ask them to mark the question they are on and then complete the section. When marking the test, you will be able to see how many questions would have been answered correctly in the time available. Repeat for the other four sections. This option is closest to the real exam.

OPTION 2: Ask your child to read through the instructions and the example at the beginning of the first section themselves. Get them to complete the practice questions and check the answer key, then allow six minutes for the 12 test questions. If they have not finished the section in the time, ask them to mark the question they are on and then complete the section. When marking the test later, you will be able to see how many questions would have been answered correctly in the time available. Repeat this process for the other four sections.

OPTION 3: Simply give the practice paper to your child and get them to read the instructions and work through the paper by themselves without any help or guidance. They should work through the questions with a clock/watch/timer to help them practise working within the allowed time. They will need to be told to ignore the instruction 'Wait until you are told to go on' written in the papers. This option would not provide any opportunity to check answers to the practice questions before working through the paper.

And finally...

Let your child know that tests are just one part of school life and that doing their best is what matters. Plan a fun incentive for after the 11+ tests, such as a day out.

Contents

Practice Test A 5

Practice Test B 21

Practice Test C 37

Practice Test D 53

Answers and Explanations 71

Practice Test A Answer Sheet 81

Practice Test B Answer Sheet 83

Practice Test C Answer Sheet 85

Practice Test D Answer Sheet 87

ACKNOWLEDGEMENTS

Every effort has been made to trace copyright holders and obtain their permission for the use of copyright material. The authors and publisher will gladly receive information enabling them to rectify any error or omission in subsequent editions. All facts are correct at time of going to press.

Published by Collins
An imprint of HarperCollins*Publishers* Limited
1 London Bridge Street
London SE1 9GF

HarperCollins*Publishers*
Macken House, 39/40 Mayor Street Upper,
Dublin 1, D01 C9W8, Ireland

ISBN 9780008761158

First published 2026

10 9 8 7 6 5 4 3 2 1

© HarperCollins*Publishers* Limited 2026

All rights reserved. No part of this publication may be reproduced, stored in a retrieval system, or transmitted, in any form or by any means, electronic, mechanical, photocopying, recording or otherwise, without the prior permission of Collins.

Without limiting the exclusive rights of any author, contributor or the publisher of this publication, any unauthorised use of this publication to train generative artificial intelligence (AI) technologies is expressly prohibited. HarperCollins also exercise their rights under Article 4(3) of the Digital Single Market Directive 2019/790 and expressly reserve this publication from the text and data mining exception.

British Library Cataloguing in Publication Data.

A CIP record of this book is available from the British Library.

Authors: Beatrix Woodhead (Tests A, B, C), Trinity Francis and Piers Knight (Test D)
Publisher: Clare Souza
Project Manager: Richard Toms
Cover Design: Sarah Duxbury and Kevin Robbins
Layout and Artwork: Ian Wrigley
Production: Bethany Brohm
Printed in India by Multivista Global Pvt. Ltd.

Non-Verbal Reasoning
Multiple-Choice Practice Test A

Read these instructions carefully.

1. You must not open or turn over this booklet until you are told to do so.

2. The booklet contains a multiple-choice test, in which you have to mark your answer to each question on the separate answer sheet.

3. There are five sections in this test. Each section starts with an explanation of what to do, followed by an example. Explanations of the answers for these are included in the answer key. You will then be asked to do two practice questions.

4. You should indicate one answer only for each question by drawing a firm pencil line clearly through the rectangle next to your answer on the answer sheet. Rub out any mistakes as well as you can and put in your new answer.

5. Complete the questions as quickly and carefully as you can. If you find that you cannot do a question, do not waste time on it but go on to the next one.

6. You should do any rough working on a separate sheet of paper.

Section 1

In each of the questions below, decide which one of the five answer options correctly shows a rotation of the figure on the left. Mark it on your answer sheet.

Here is an example to help you.

Example

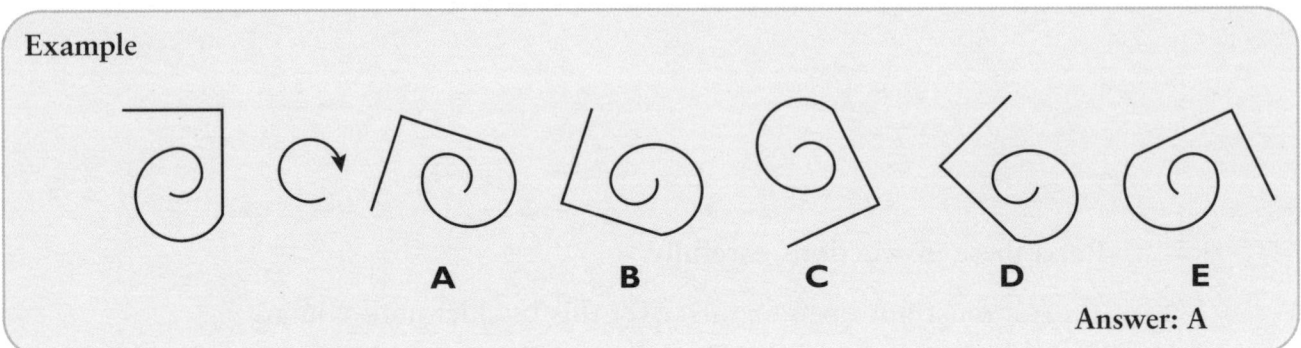

Answer: A

Now try these practice questions.

P1.

P2.

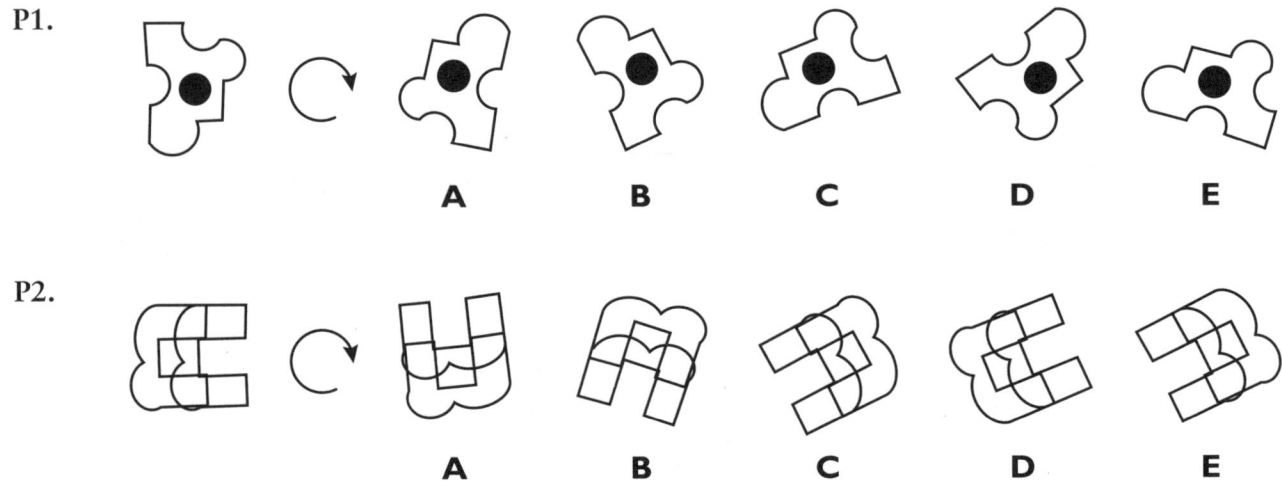

WAIT UNTIL YOU ARE TOLD TO GO ON

1.

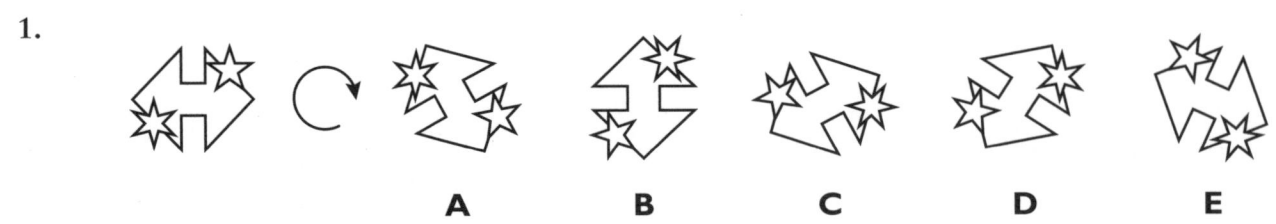

NOW GO ON TO THE NEXT PAGE

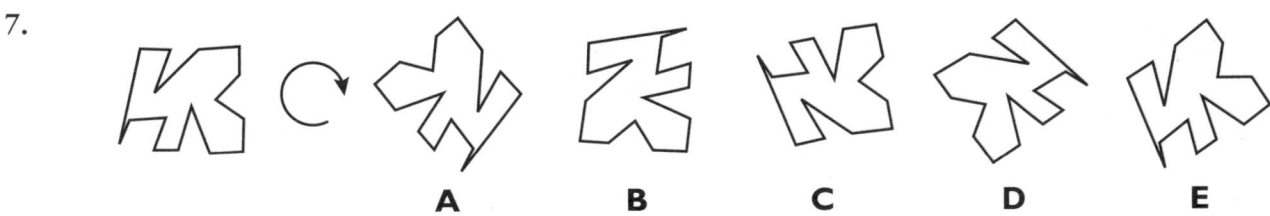

8.

9.

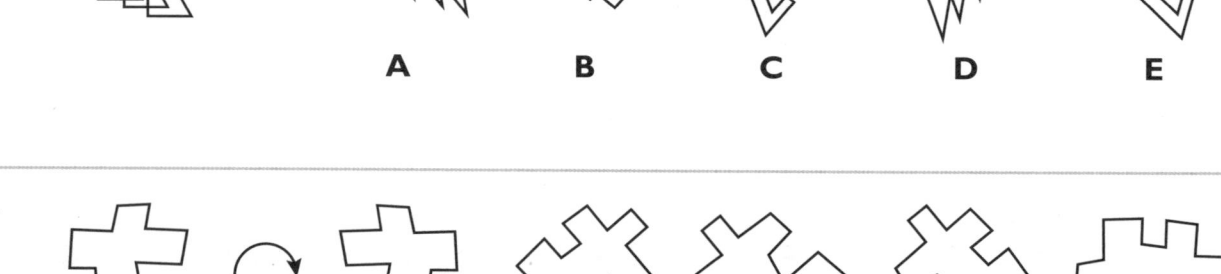

10.

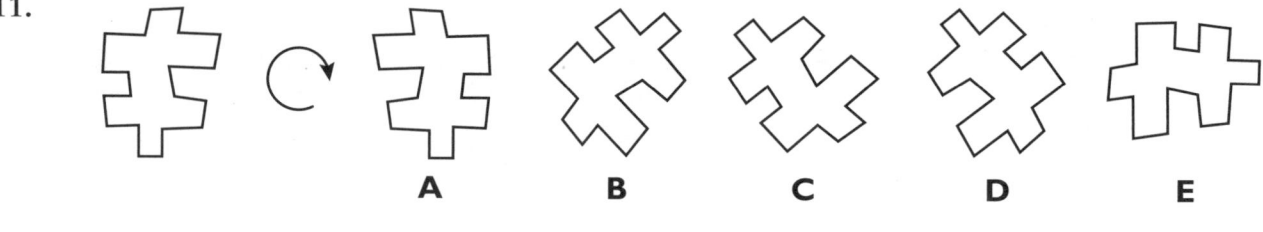

11.

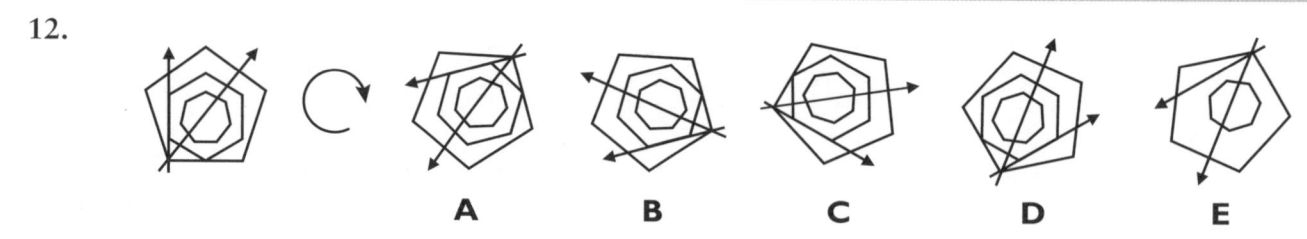

12.

WAIT UNTIL YOU ARE TOLD TO GO ON

Section 2

In the grids below, one square has been left empty. Look carefully at the five squares to the right and select the square that should complete the grid. Mark it on your answer sheet.

Here is an example to help you.

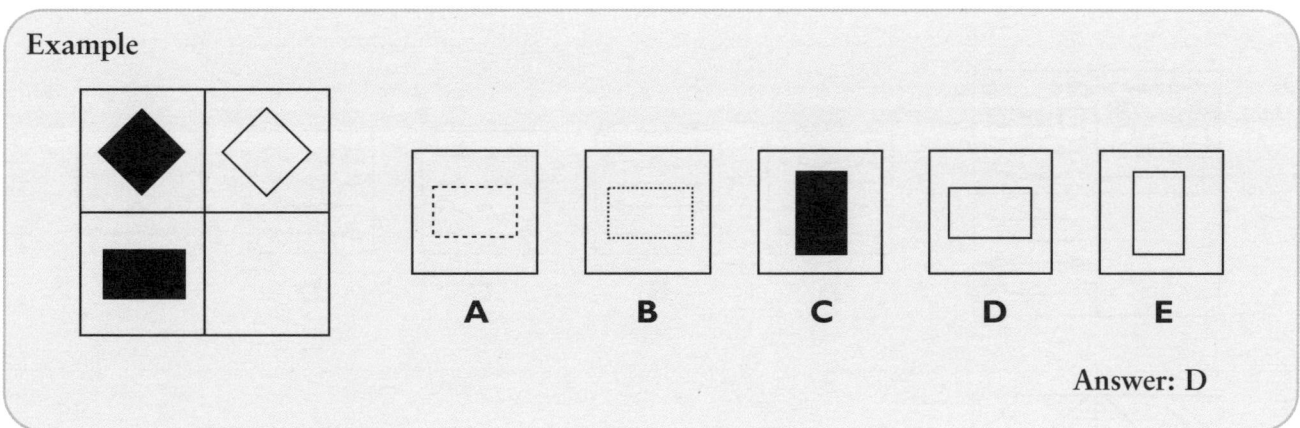

Now try these practice questions.

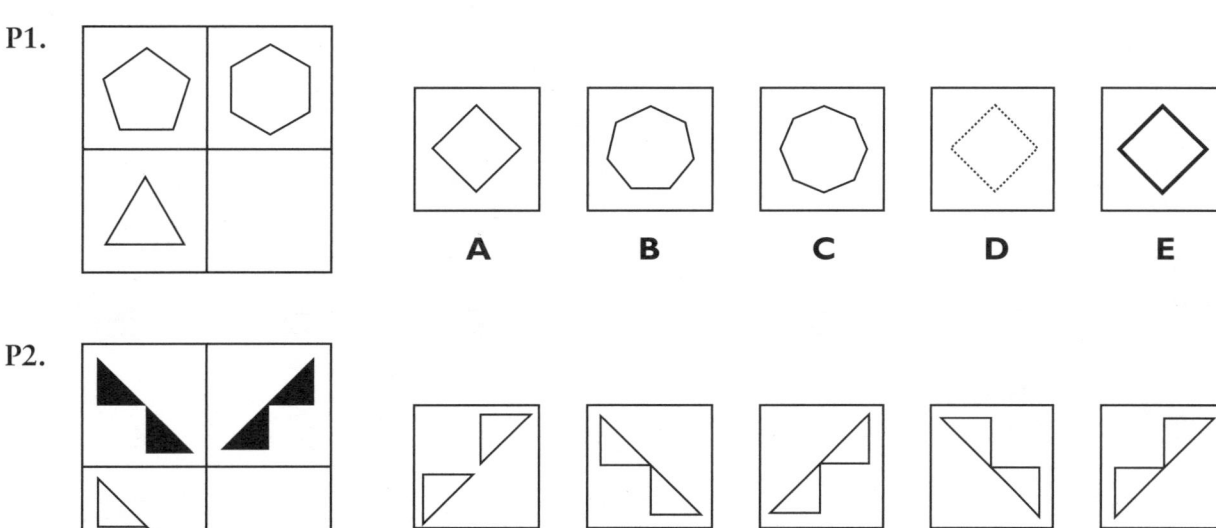

WAIT UNTIL YOU ARE TOLD TO GO ON

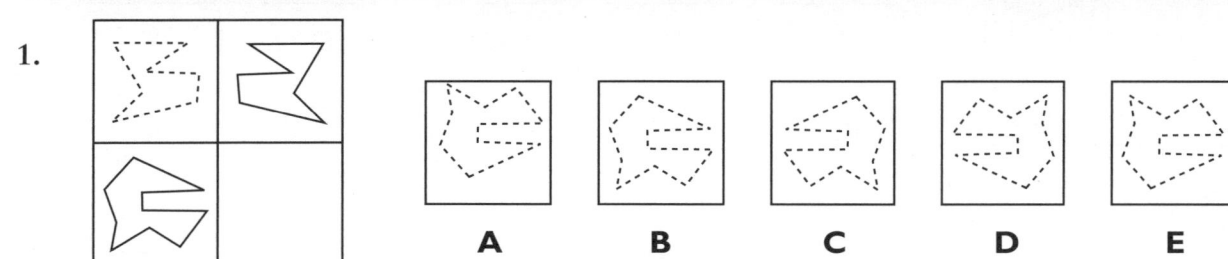

NOW GO ON TO THE NEXT PAGE

2.

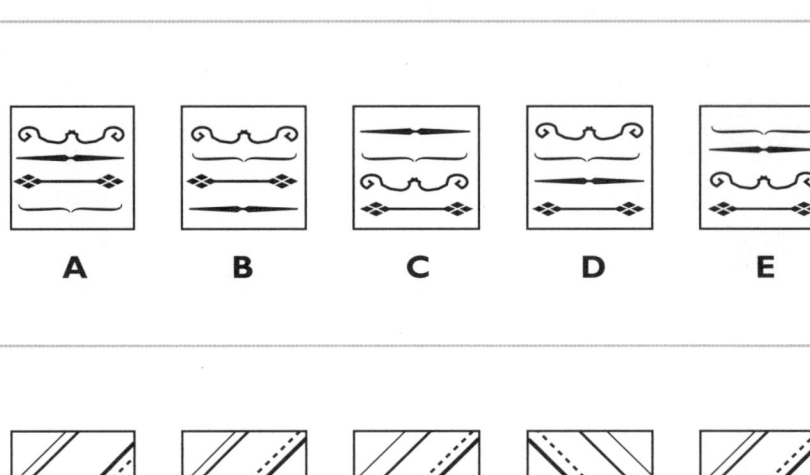

3.

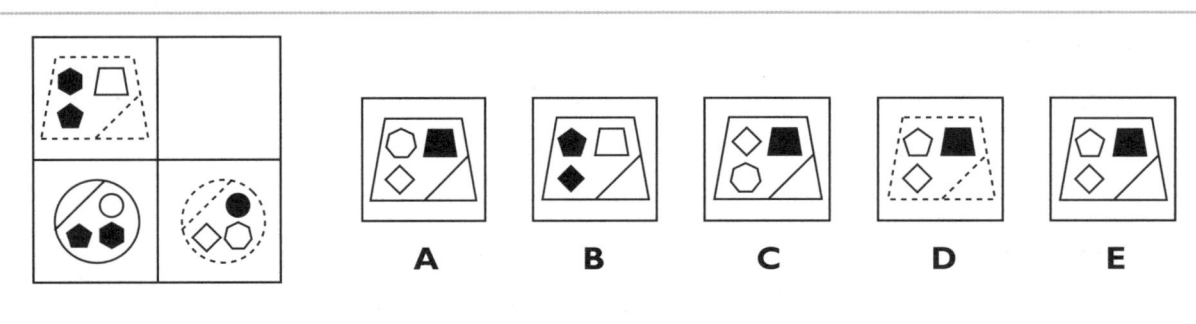

4.

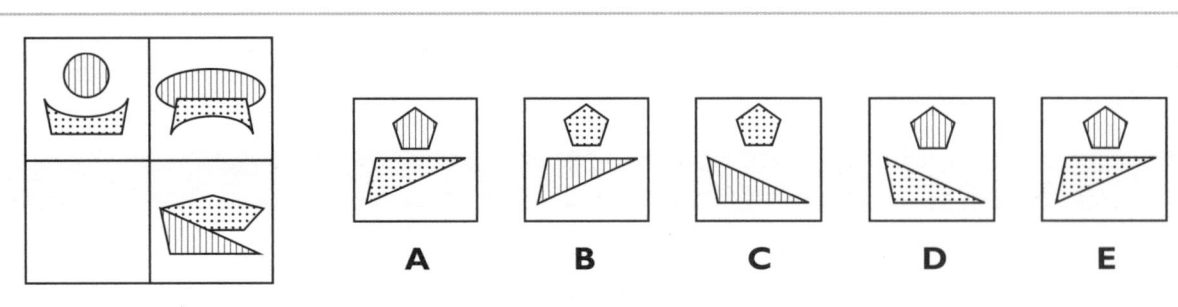

5.

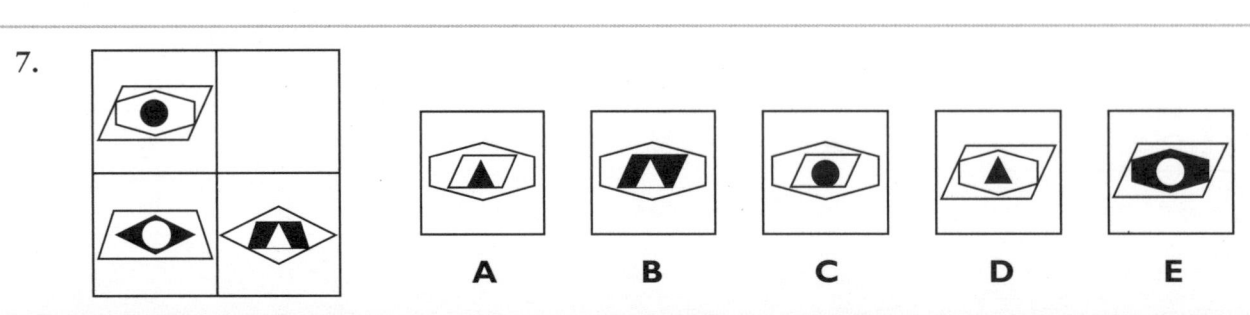

8.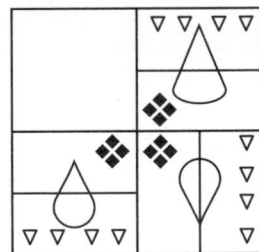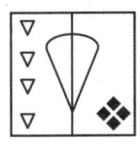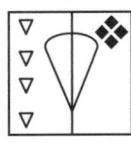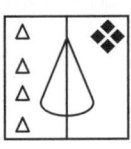

A B C D E

9.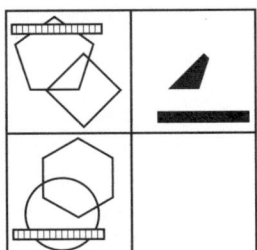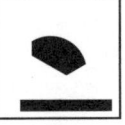

A B C D E

10.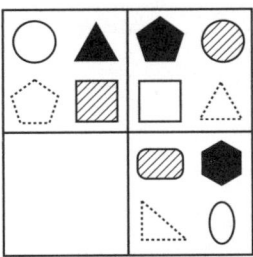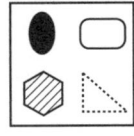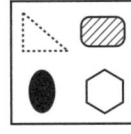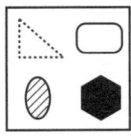

A B C D E

11.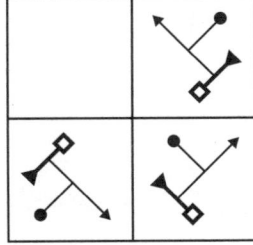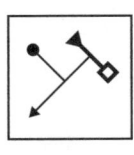

A B C D E

12.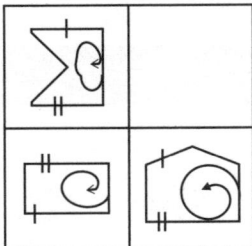

A B C D E

WAIT UNTIL YOU ARE TOLD TO GO ON

Section 3

In each question, there are two figures on the left with an arrow between them. Look at them carefully and decide how the second figure is related to the first figure. There is then a third figure and another arrow followed by five more figures. Decide which one of the five figures completes the second pair in the same way as the first pair. Mark it on your answer sheet.

Here is an example to help you.

Example

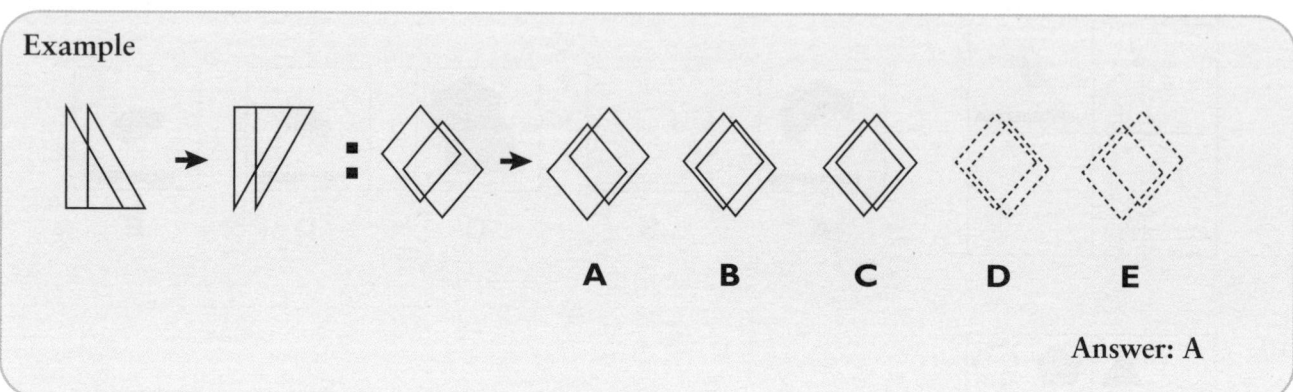

Answer: A

Now try these practice questions.

P1.

P2.

WAIT UNTIL YOU ARE TOLD TO GO ON

1.

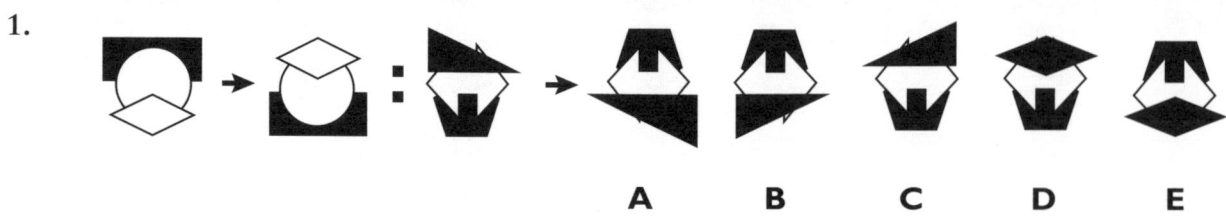

NOW GO ON TO THE NEXT PAGE

2.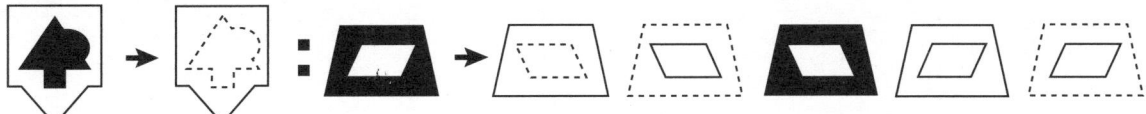

3.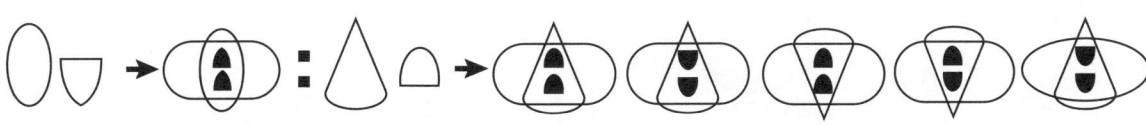

4.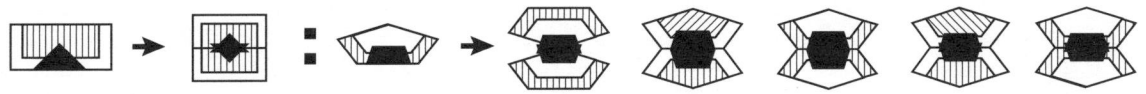

5.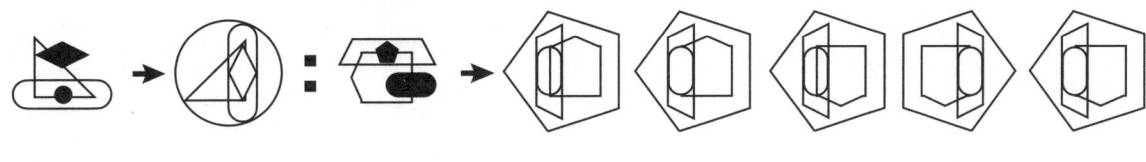

6.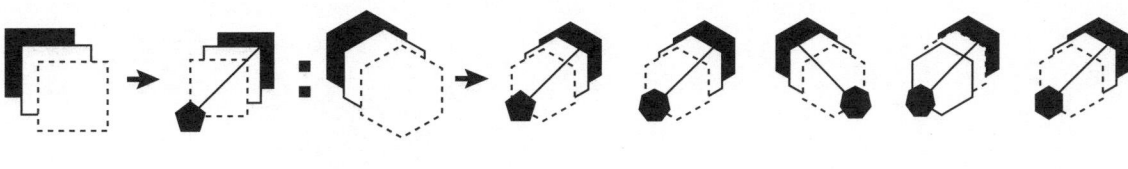

7.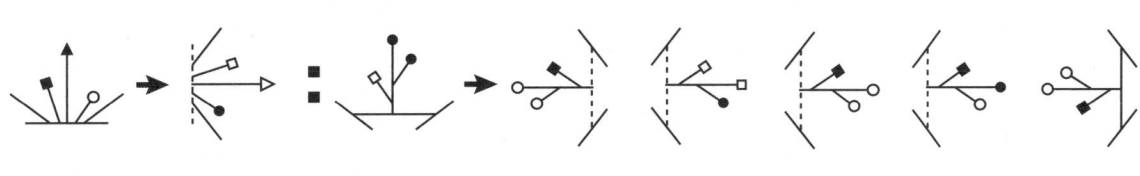

8.

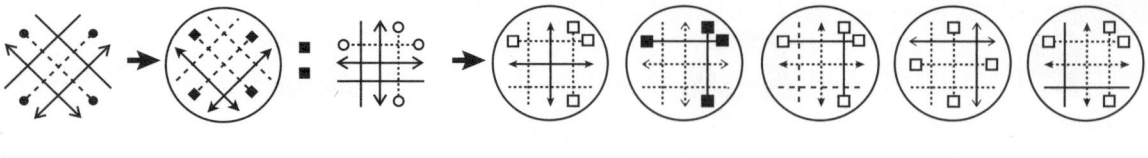

A B C D E

9.

A B C D E

10.

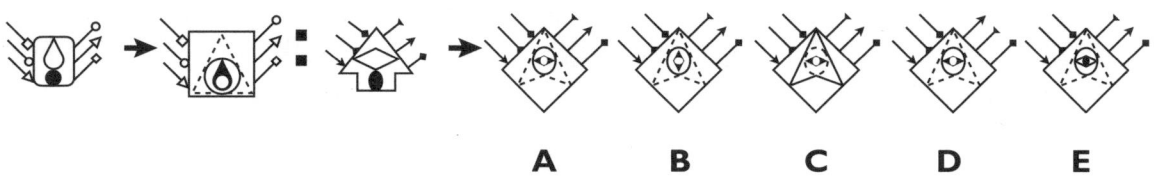

A B C D E

11.

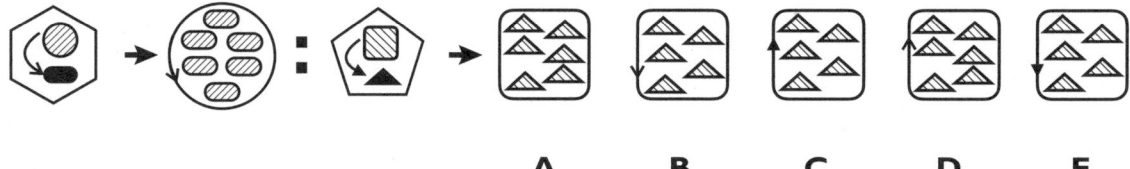

A B C D E

12.

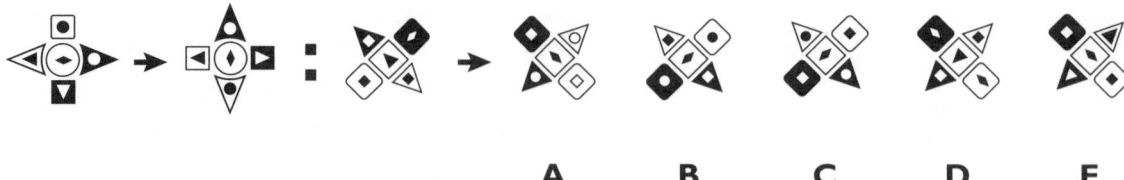

A B C D E

WAIT UNTIL YOU ARE TOLD TO GO ON

Section 4

Look at the given net on the left. Work out which one of the cubes on the right can be made using that net. Mark it on your answer sheet.

Here is an example to help you.

Example

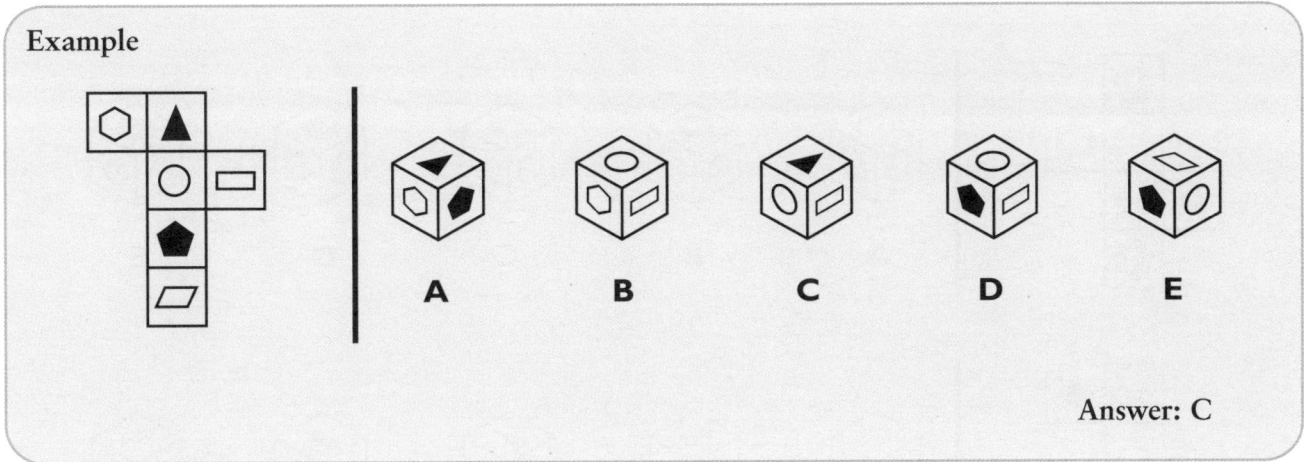

Answer: C

Now try these practice questions.

P1.

                    A   B   C   D   E

P2.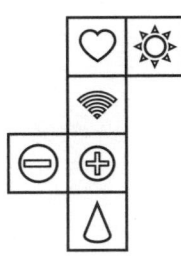

                    A   B   C   D   E

WAIT UNTIL YOU ARE TOLD TO GO ON

NOW GO ON TO THE NEXT PAGE

1.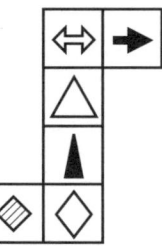
                             A   B   C   D   E

2.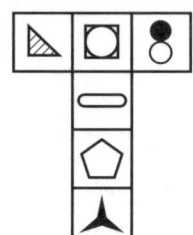
                             A   B   C   D   E

3.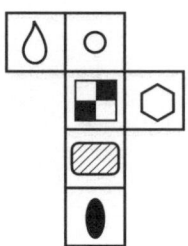
                             A   B   C   D   E

4.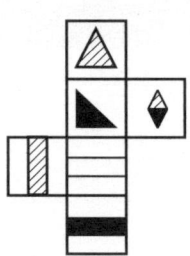
                             A   B   C   D   E

5.
                             A   B   C   D   E

6.
                             A   B   C   D   E

NOW GO ON TO THE NEXT PAGE

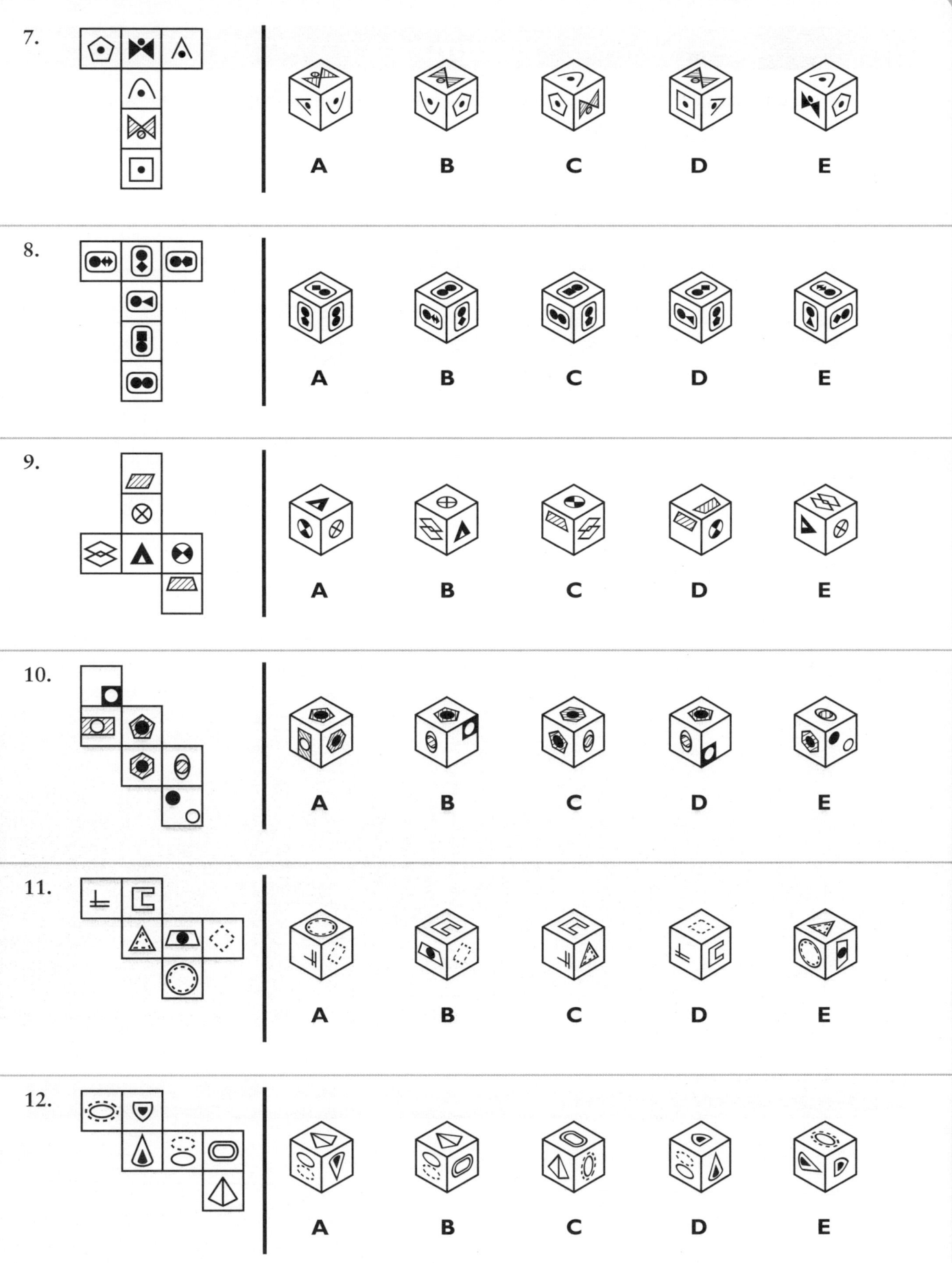

Section 5

The following questions are about finding the odd one out in a series of shapes or patterns. Find the odd one out and mark it on your answer sheet.

Here is an example to help you.

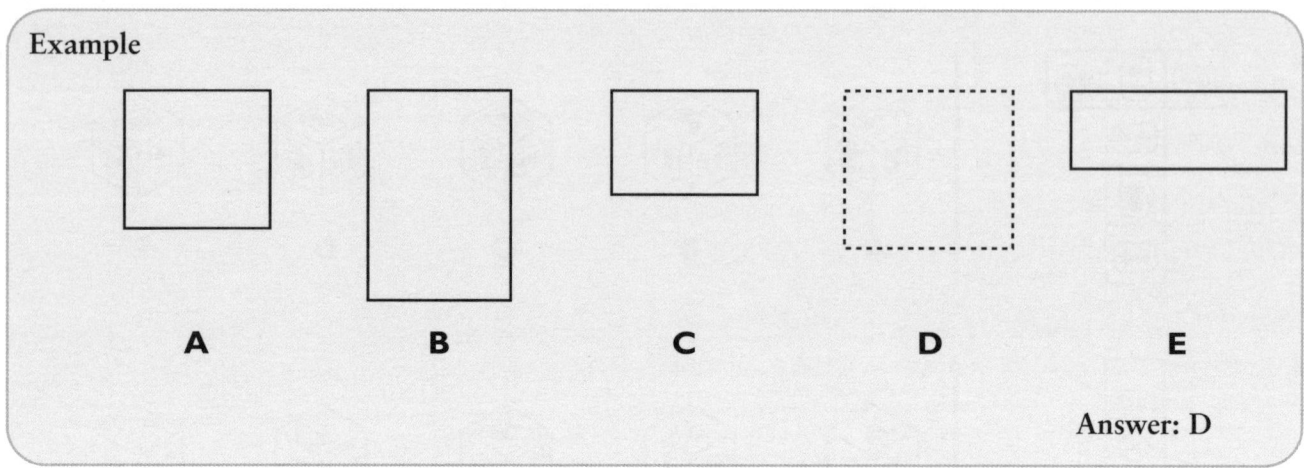

Answer: D

Now try these practice questions.

P1.

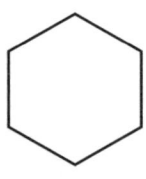 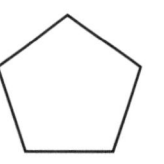  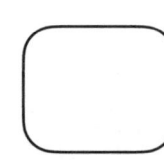

A　　　　　B　　　　　C　　　　　D　　　　　E

P2.

  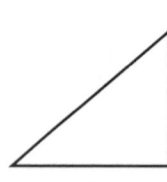 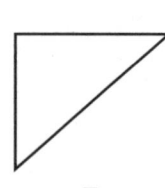 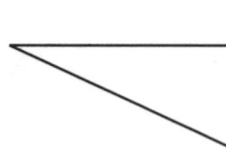

A　　　　　B　　　　　C　　　　　D　　　　　E

WAIT UNTIL YOU ARE TOLD TO GO ON

NOW GO ON TO THE NEXT PAGE

1.

| A | B | C | D | E |

2.

| A | B | C | D | E |

3.

| A | B | C | D | E |

4.

| A | B | C | D | E |

5.

| A | B | C | D | E |

6.

| A | B | C | D | E |

NOW GO ON TO THE NEXT PAGE

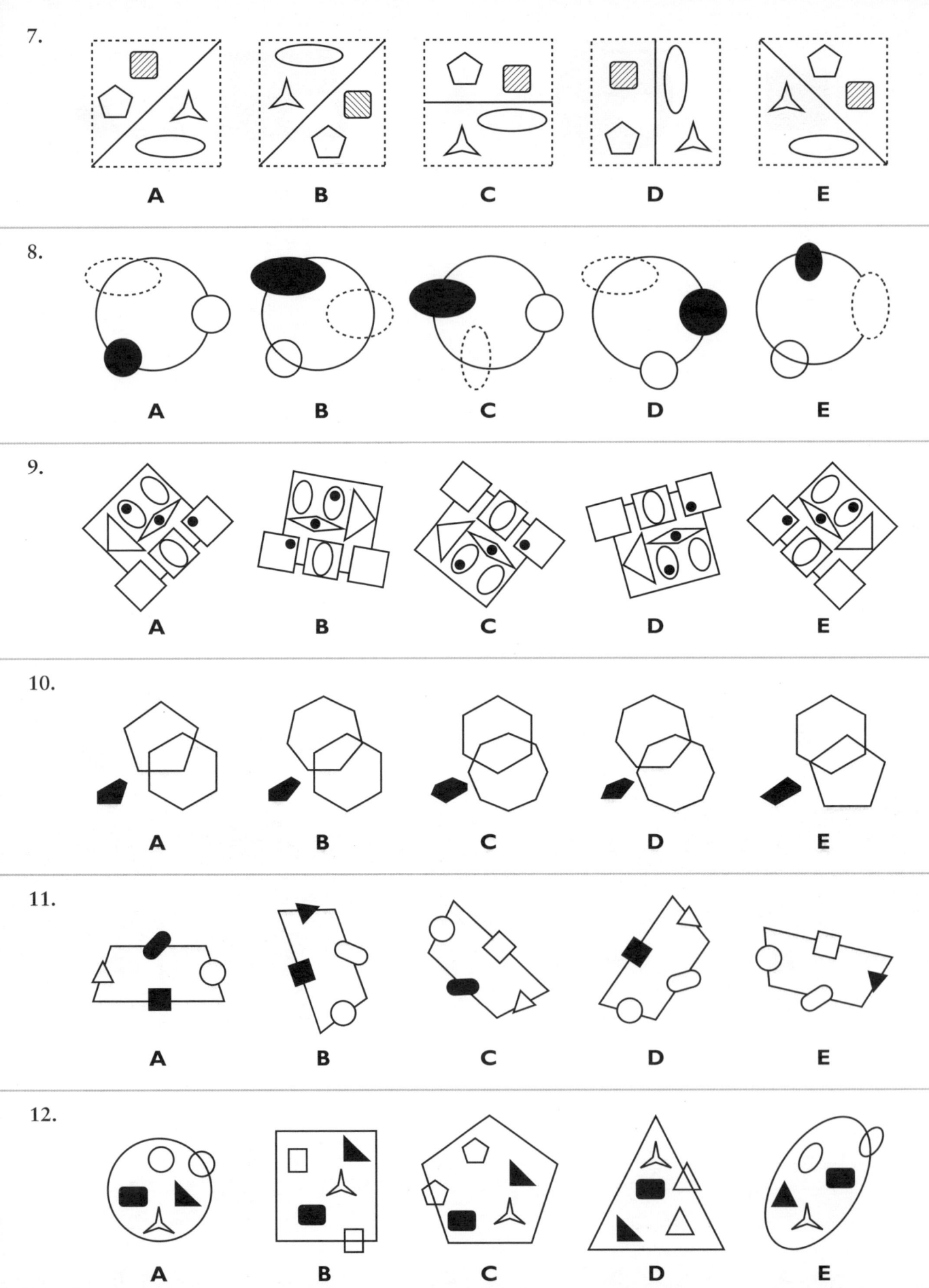

Non-Verbal Reasoning
Multiple-Choice Practice Test B

Read these instructions carefully.

1. You must not open or turn over this booklet until you are told to do so.

2. The booklet contains a multiple-choice test, in which you have to mark your answer to each question on the separate answer sheet.

3. There are five sections in this test. Each section starts with an explanation of what to do, followed by an example. Explanations of the answers for these are included in the answer key. You will then be asked to do two practice questions.

4. You should indicate one answer only for each question by drawing a firm pencil line clearly through the rectangle next to your answer on the answer sheet. Rub out any mistakes as well as you can and put in your new answer.

5. Complete the questions as quickly and carefully as you can. If you find that you cannot do a question, do not waste time on it but go on to the next one.

6. You should do any rough working on a separate sheet of paper.

Section 1

In the questions below, you have to work out a code. You are given some figures and the codes that go with them. Decide how the codes match the figures. Then look at the test figure and find its correct code from the five given on the right. Mark it on your answer sheet.

Here is an example to help you.

Example

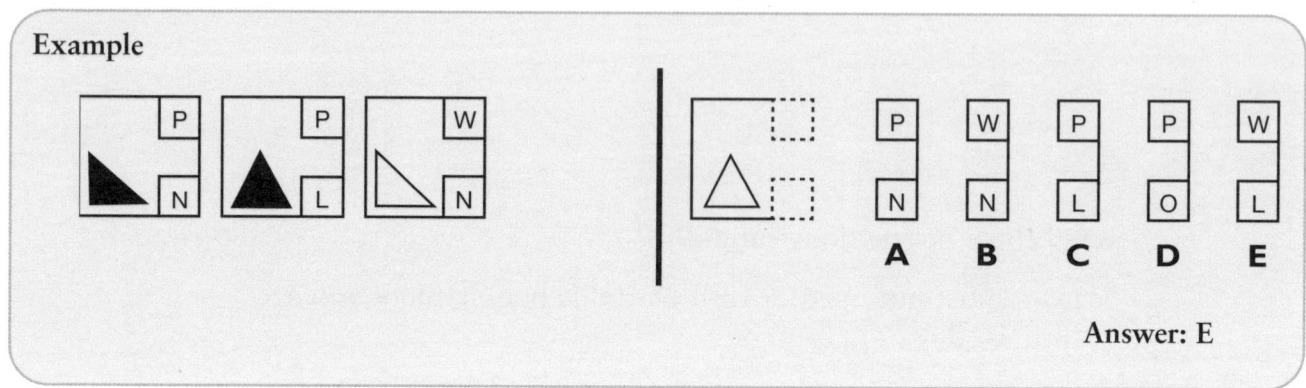

Answer: E

Now try these practice questions.

P1.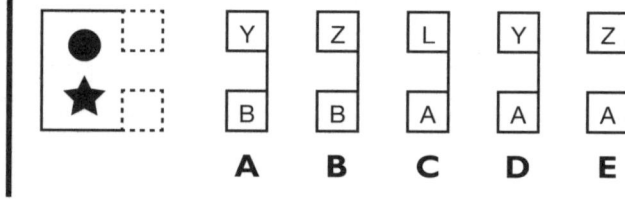

P2.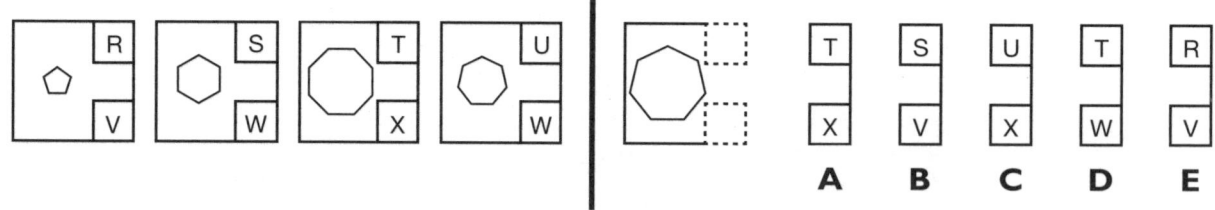

WAIT UNTIL YOU ARE TOLD TO GO ON

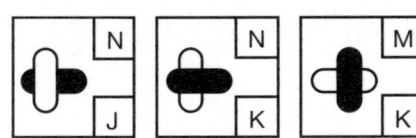

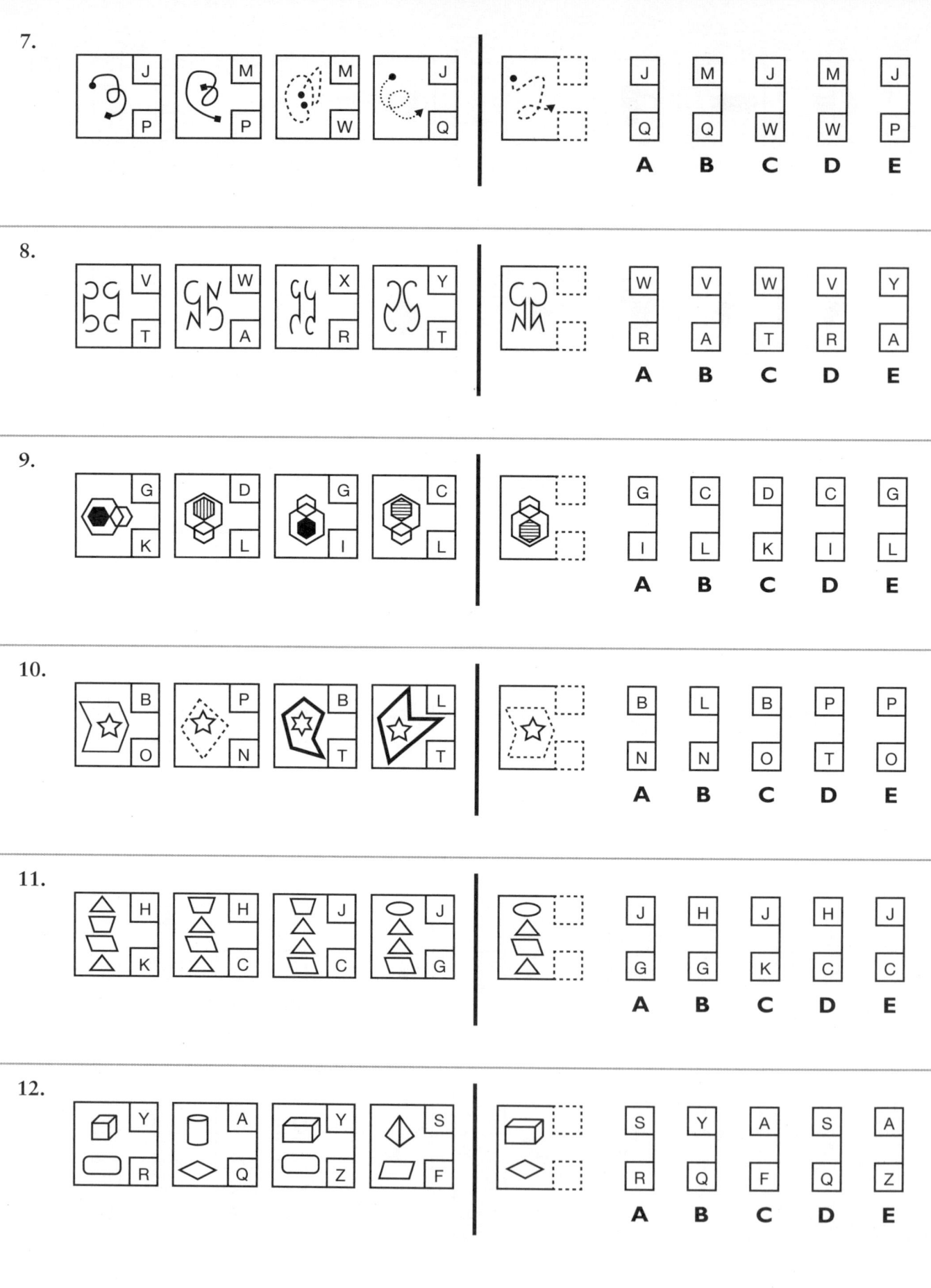

Section 2

In each question, two figures are brought together, without being rotated or reflected, to create a new figure. Decide which option shows the correct figure and mark it on your answer sheet.

Here is an example to help you.

Example

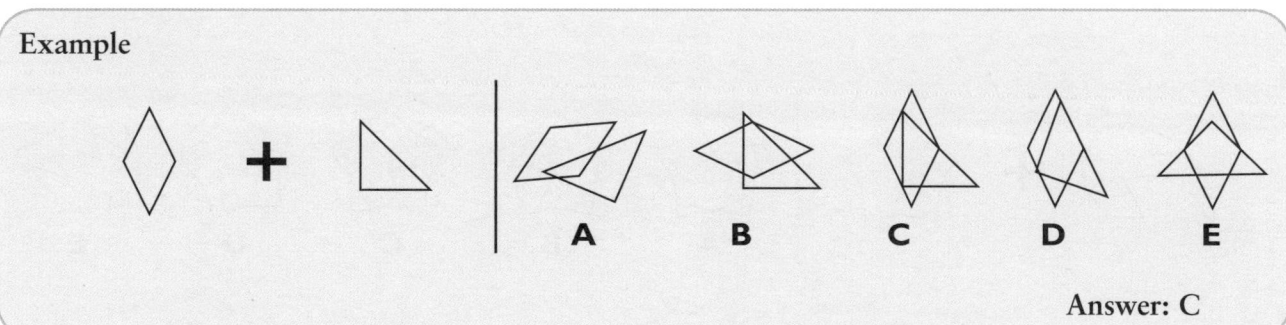

Answer: C

Now try these practice questions.

P1.

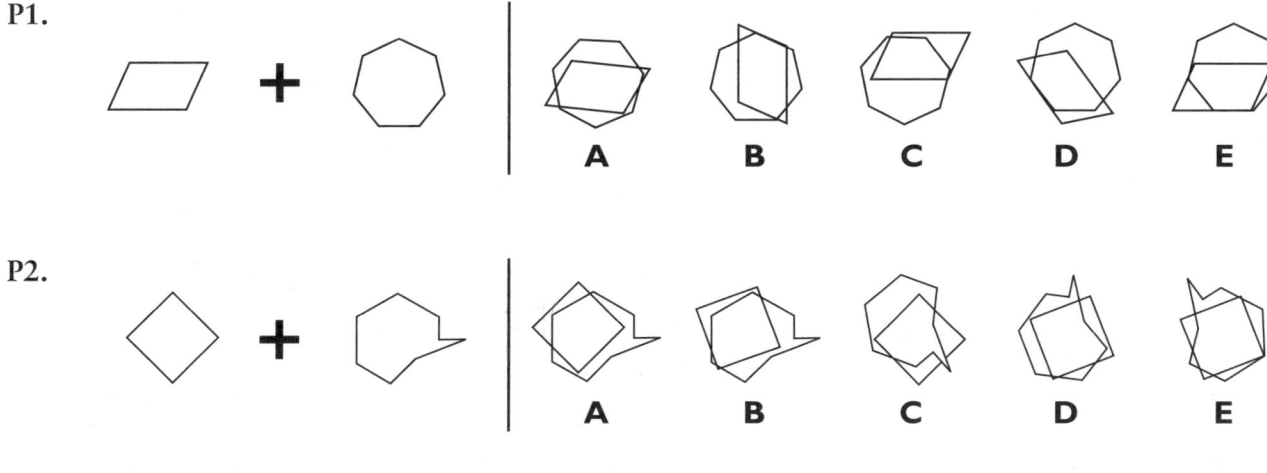

P2.

WAIT UNTIL YOU ARE TOLD TO GO ON

1.

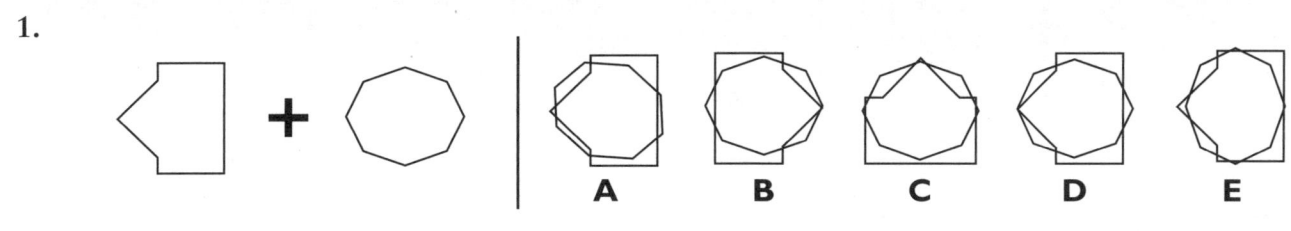

2.

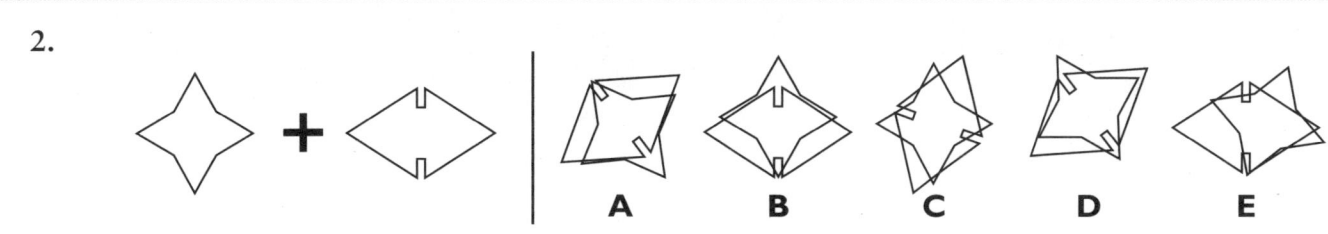

NOW GO ON TO THE NEXT PAGE

3.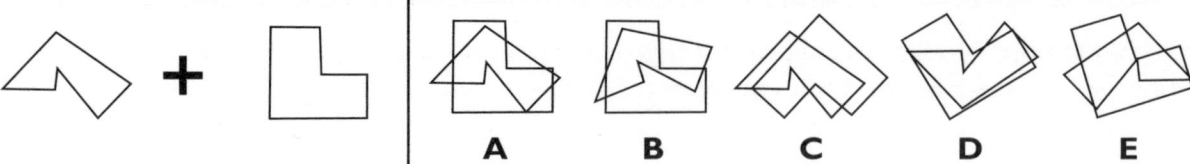

4.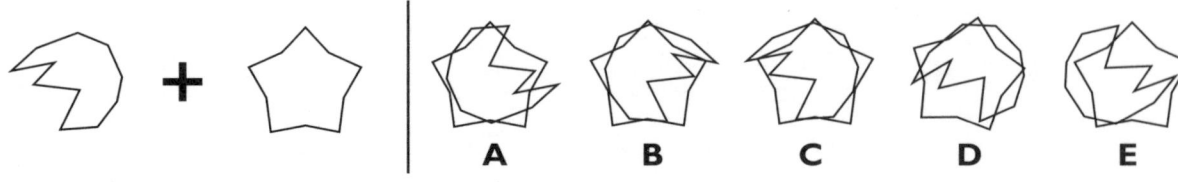

5.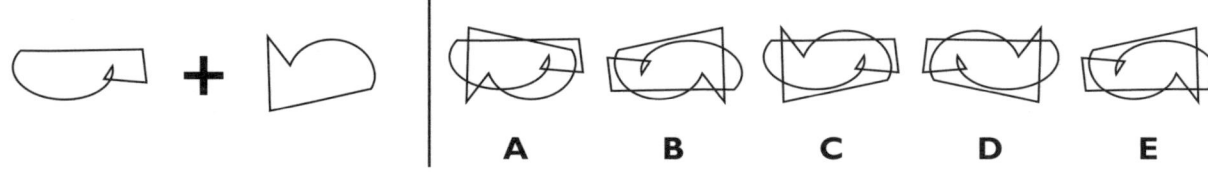

6.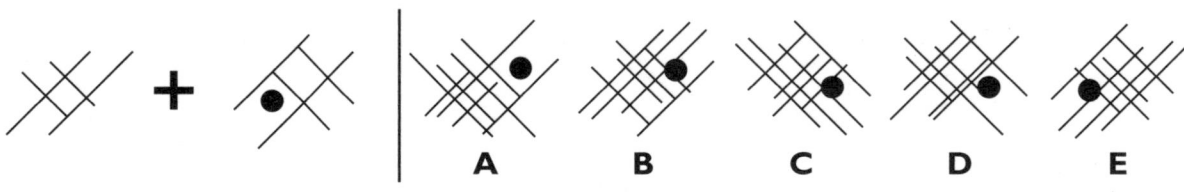

7.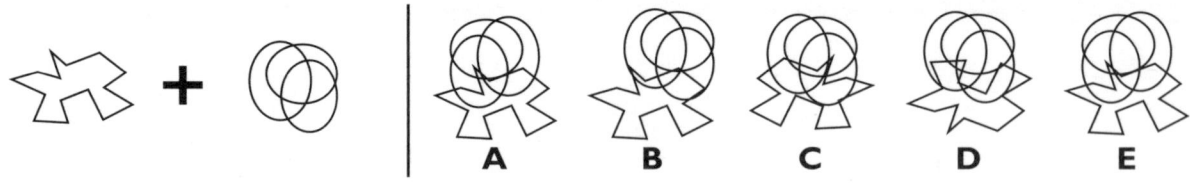

8.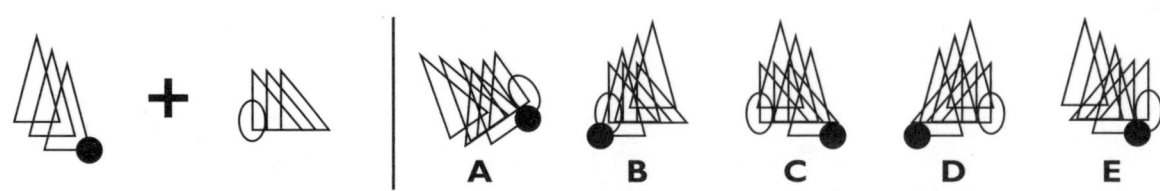

NOW GO ON TO THE NEXT PAGE

9.
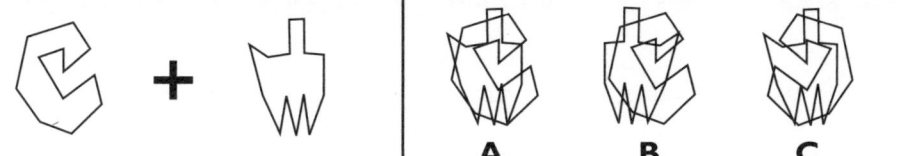

10.
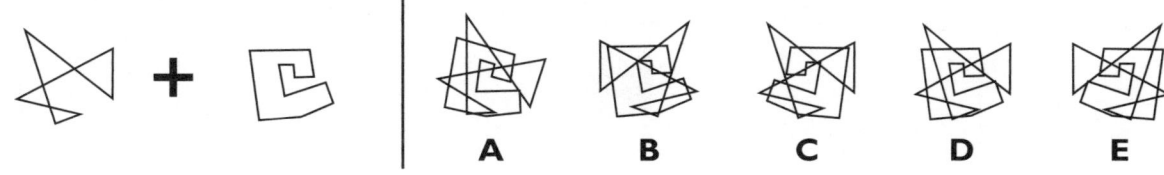

11.
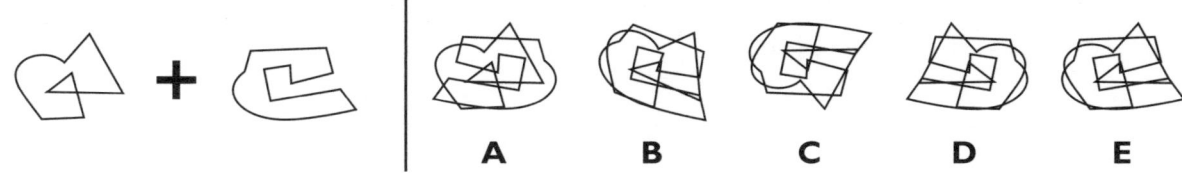

12.
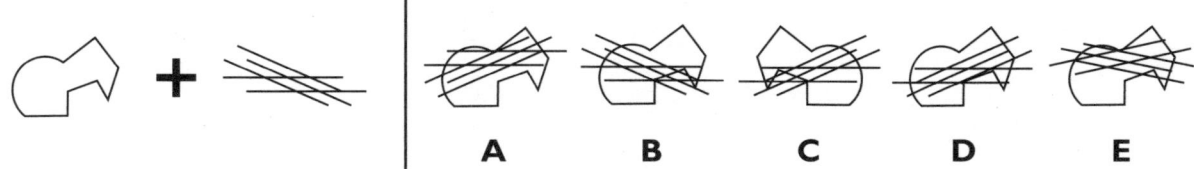

WAIT UNTIL YOU ARE TOLD TO GO ON

Section 3

In each question, two figures are shown on the left. They have something in common. Decide which of the options on the right is most like the figures on the left and mark its letter on your answer sheet.

Here is an example to help you.

Example

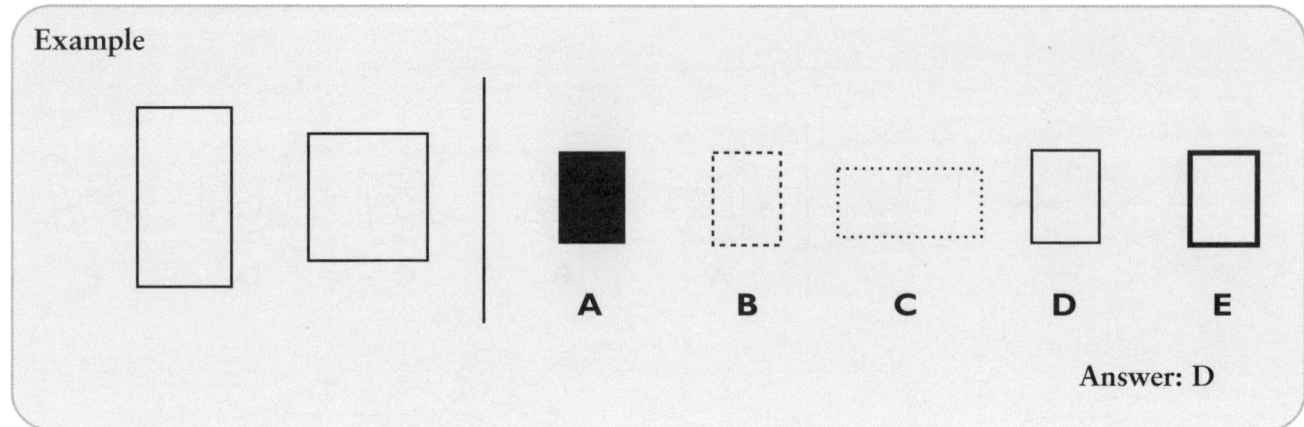

Answer: D

Now try these practice questions.

P1.

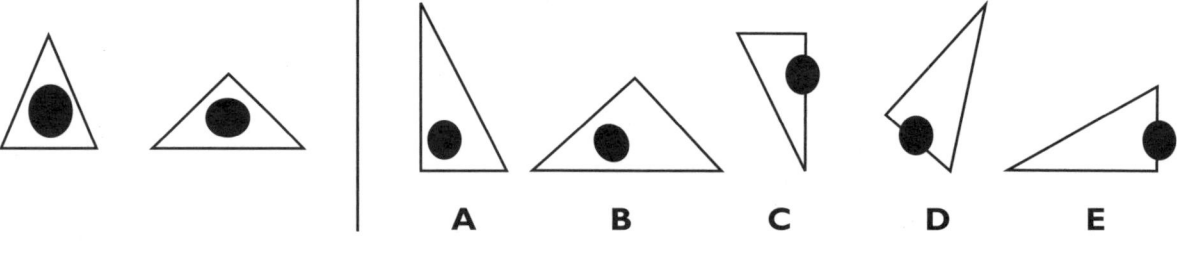

P2.

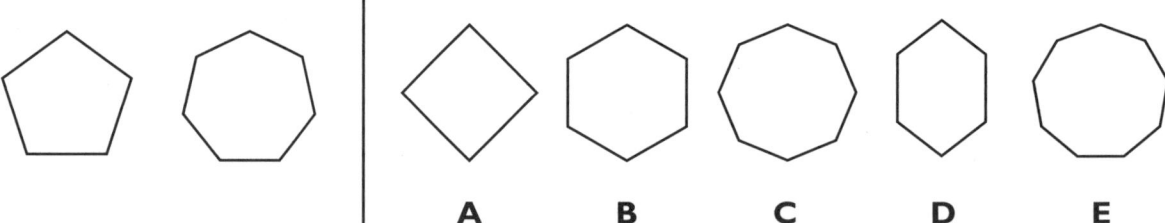

WAIT UNTIL YOU ARE TOLD TO GO ON

NOW GO ON TO THE NEXT PAGE

1.

7.

8.

9.

10.

11.

12.

WAIT UNTIL YOU ARE TOLD TO GO ON

Section 4

In each question, the blocks are all the same size and shape. Some blocks may be hidden from view, supporting blocks above. Decide which option correctly shows how many blocks are in the diagram and mark its letter on your answer sheet.

Here is an example to help you.

Example

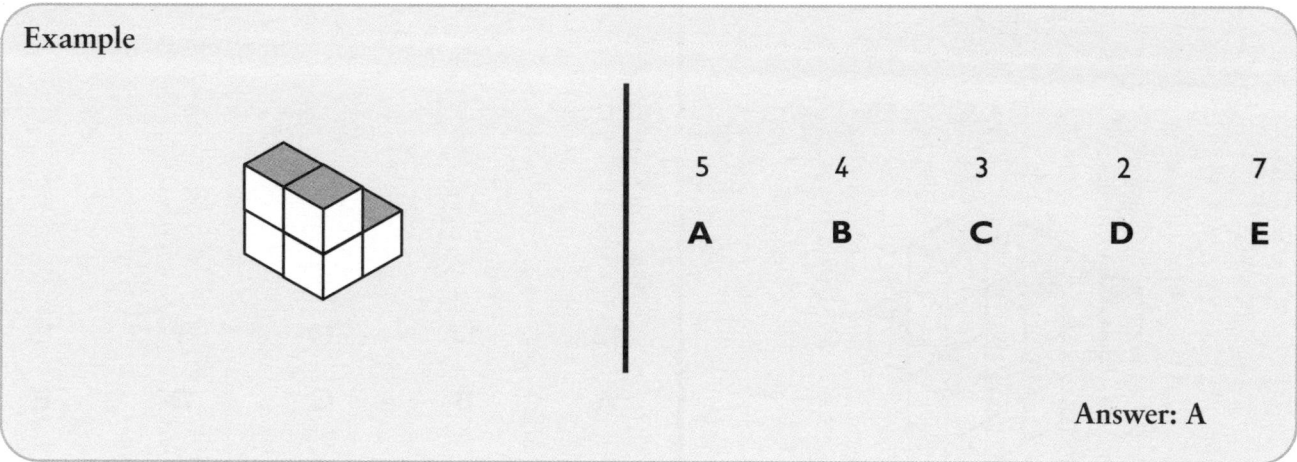

5	4	3	2	7
A	B	C	D	E

Answer: A

Now try these practice questions.

P1.

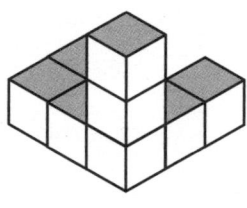

8	5	10	6	7
A	B	C	D	E

P2.

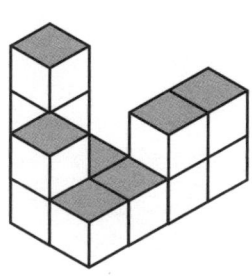

14	13	11	12	10
A	B	C	D	E

WAIT UNTIL YOU ARE TOLD TO GO ON

NOW GO ON TO THE NEXT PAGE

1.

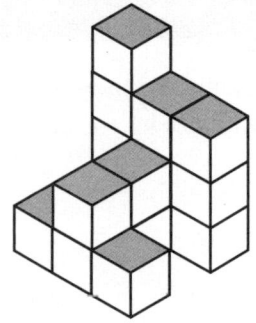

17	11	16	12	13
A	**B**	**C**	**D**	**E**

2.

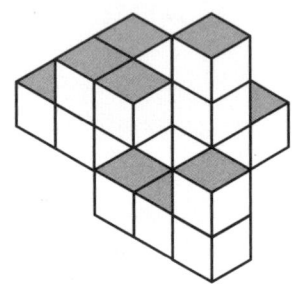

12	13	14	9	15
A	**B**	**C**	**D**	**E**

3.

14	13	15	12	16
A	**B**	**C**	**D**	**E**

4.

15	17	13	14	16
A	**B**	**C**	**D**	**E**

NOW GO ON TO THE NEXT PAGE

5.

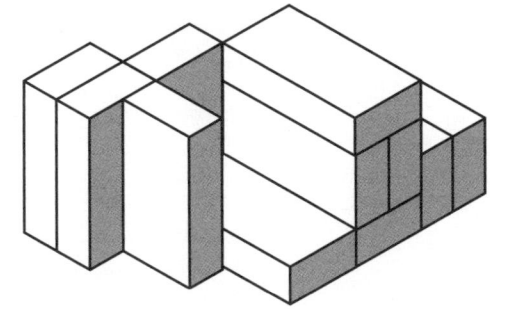

10	11	13	12	9
A	**B**	**C**	**D**	**E**

6.

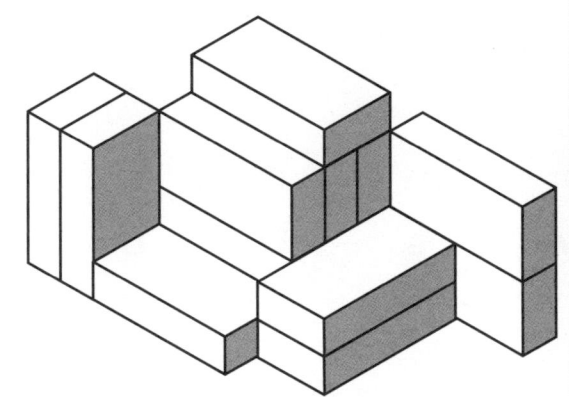

14	12	15	11	13
A	**B**	**C**	**D**	**E**

7.

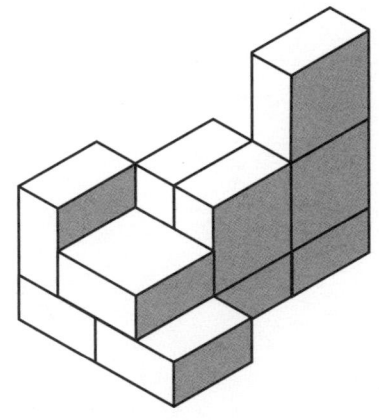

11	10	9	12	13
A	**B**	**C**	**D**	**E**

8.

23	18	25	16	20
A	**B**	**C**	**D**	**E**

NOW GO ON TO THE NEXT PAGE

9.

15	13	19	17	16
A	**B**	**C**	**D**	**E**

10.

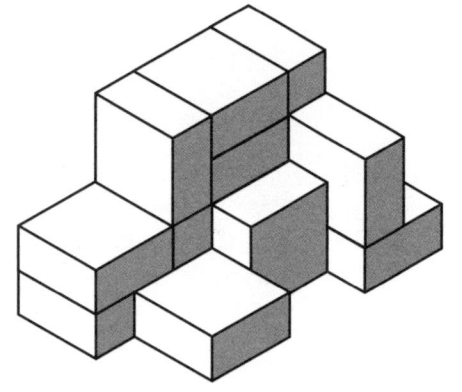

14	12	11	10	13
A	**B**	**C**	**D**	**E**

11.

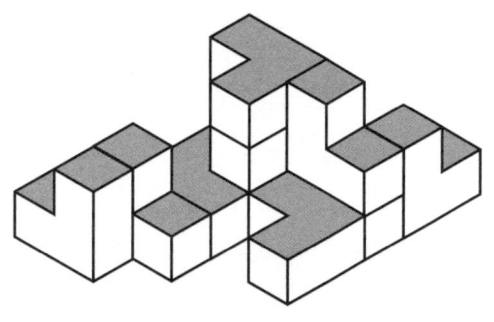

7	10	8	12	9
A	**B**	**C**	**D**	**E**

12.

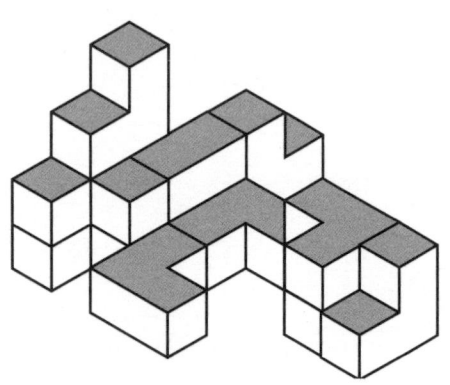

9	12	11	13	10
A	**B**	**C**	**D**	**E**

WAIT UNTIL YOU ARE TOLD TO GO ON

Section 5

In each question, there is a sequence of triangles with one left empty. Decide which triangle on the right completes the sequence and mark its letter on your answer sheet.

Here is an example to help you.

Example

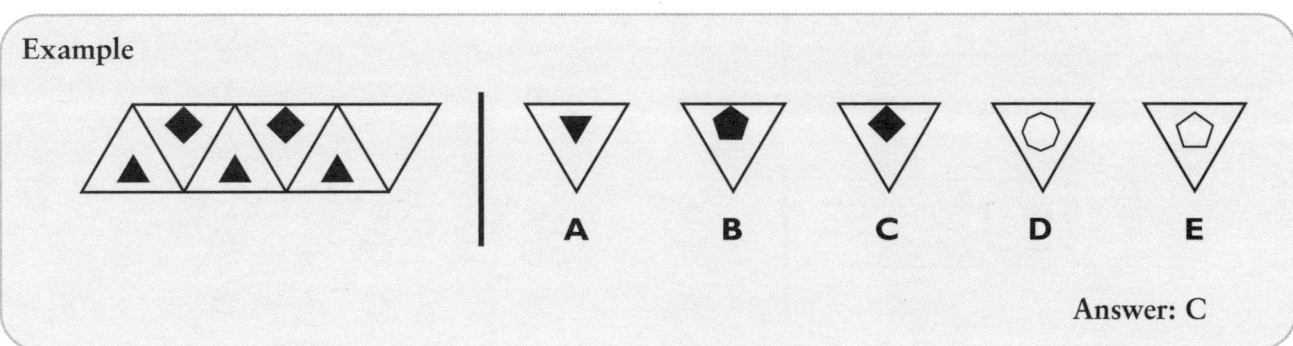

Answer: C

Now try these practice questions.

P1.

P2.

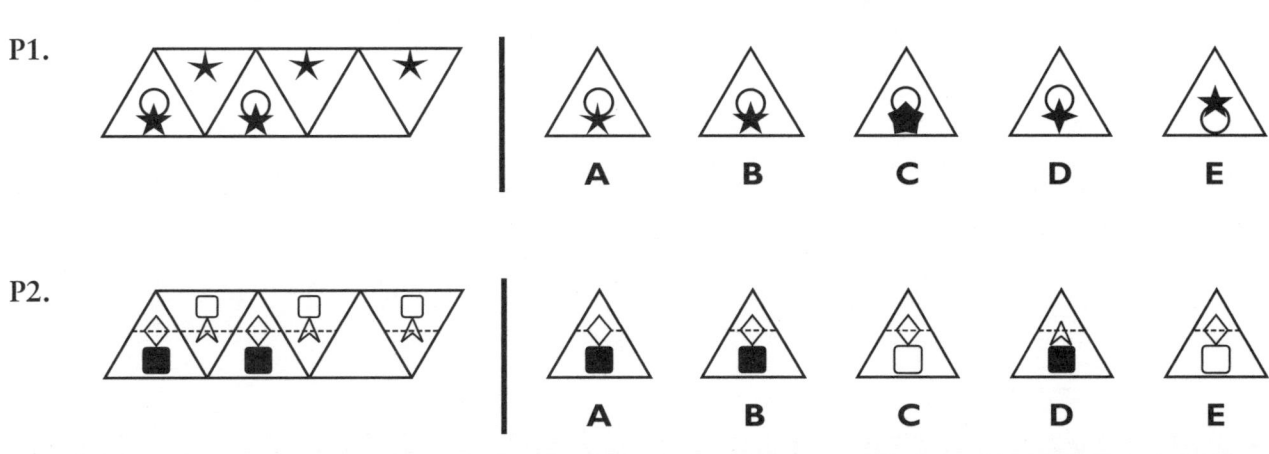

WAIT UNTIL YOU ARE TOLD TO GO ON

1.

2.

3.

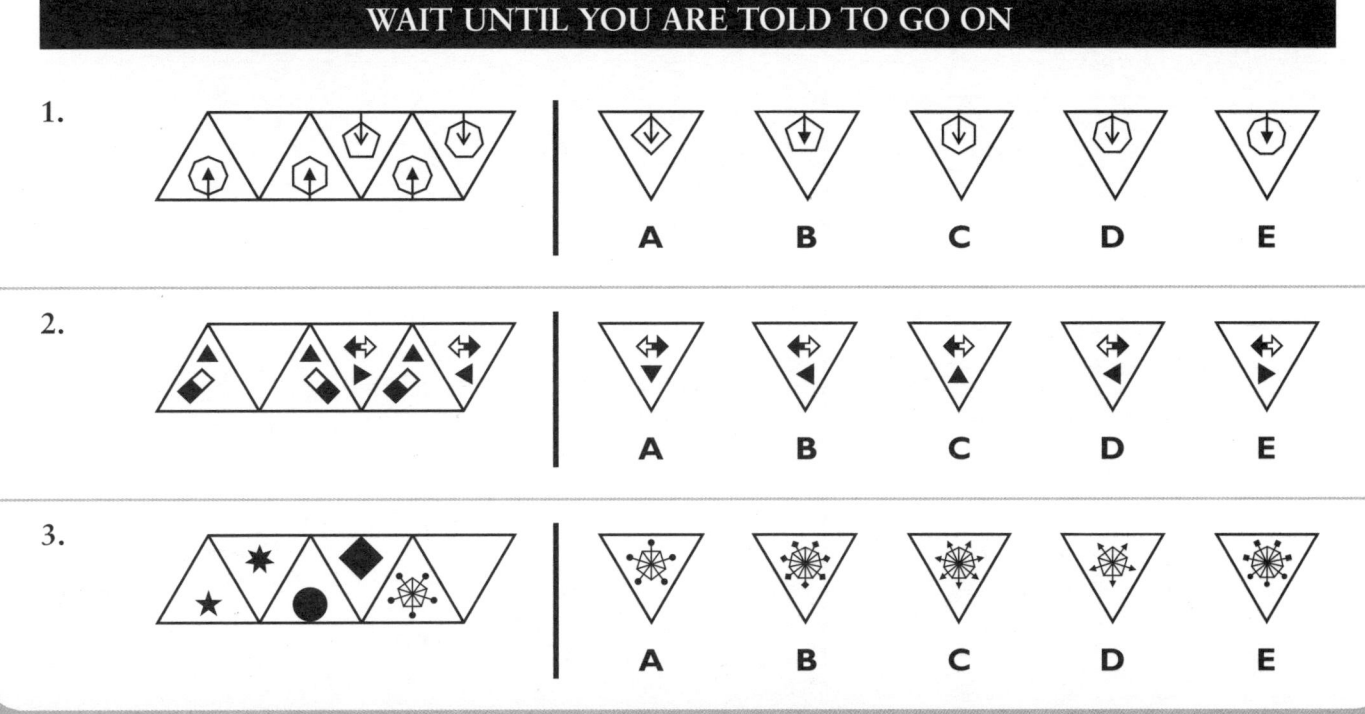

NOW GO ON TO THE NEXT PAGE

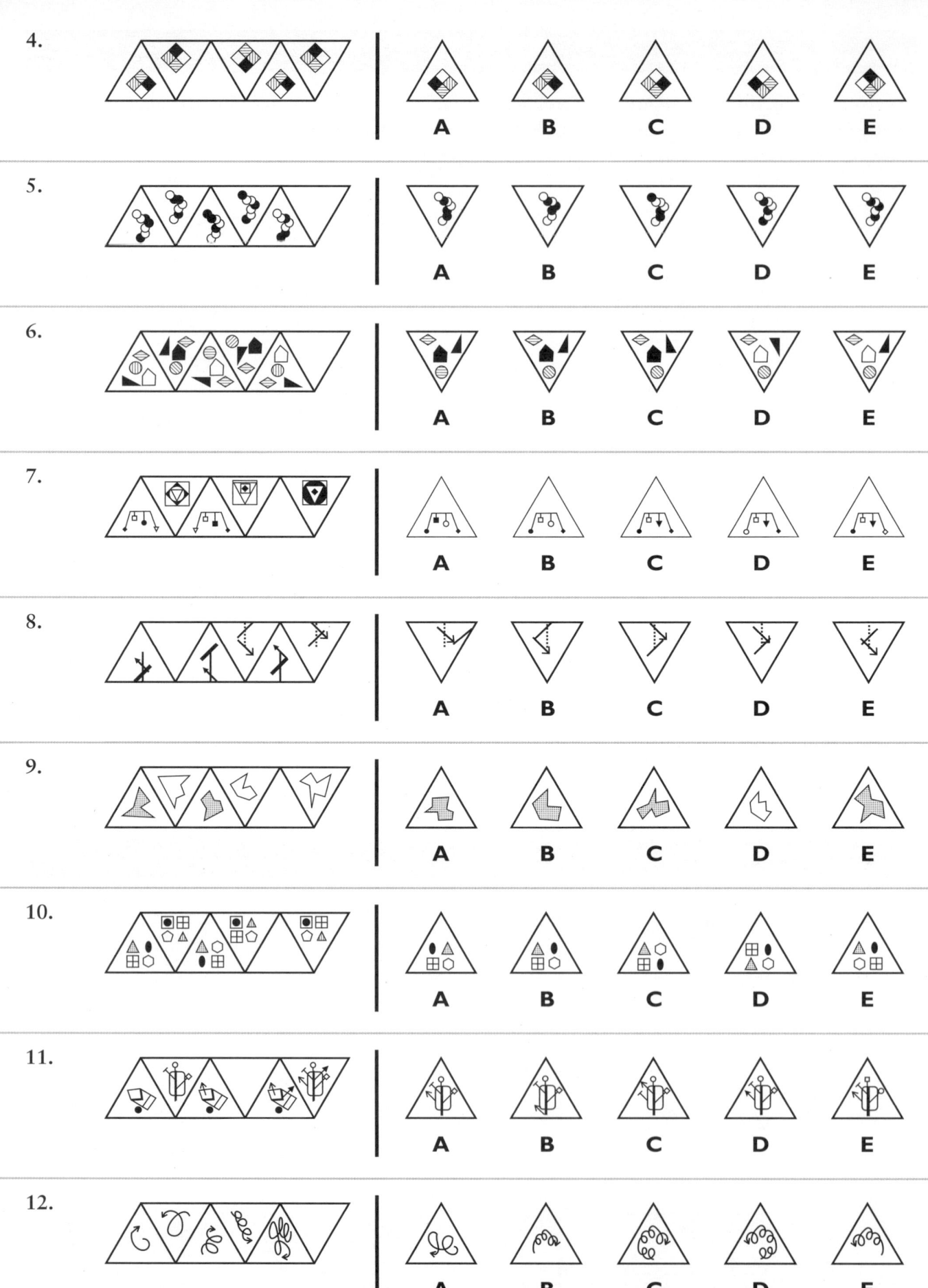

Non-Verbal Reasoning
Multiple-Choice Practice Test C

Read these instructions carefully.

1. You must not open or turn over this booklet until you are told to do so.

2. The booklet contains a multiple-choice test, in which you have to mark your answer to each question on the separate answer sheet.

3. There are five sections in this test. Each section starts with an explanation of what to do, followed by an example. Explanations of the answers for these are included in the answer key. You will then be asked to do two practice questions.

4. You should indicate one answer only for each question by drawing a firm pencil line clearly through the rectangle next to your answer on the answer sheet. Rub out any mistakes as well as you can and put in your new answer.

5. Complete the questions as quickly and carefully as you can. If you find that you cannot do a question, do not waste time on it but go on to the next one.

6. You should do any rough working on a separate sheet of paper.

Section 1

In each question, there are two figures on the left with an arrow between them. Look at them carefully and decide how the second figure is related to the first figure. There is then a third figure and another arrow followed by five more figures. Decide which one of the five figures completes the second pair in the same way as the first pair. Mark it on your answer sheet.

Here is an example to help you.

Example

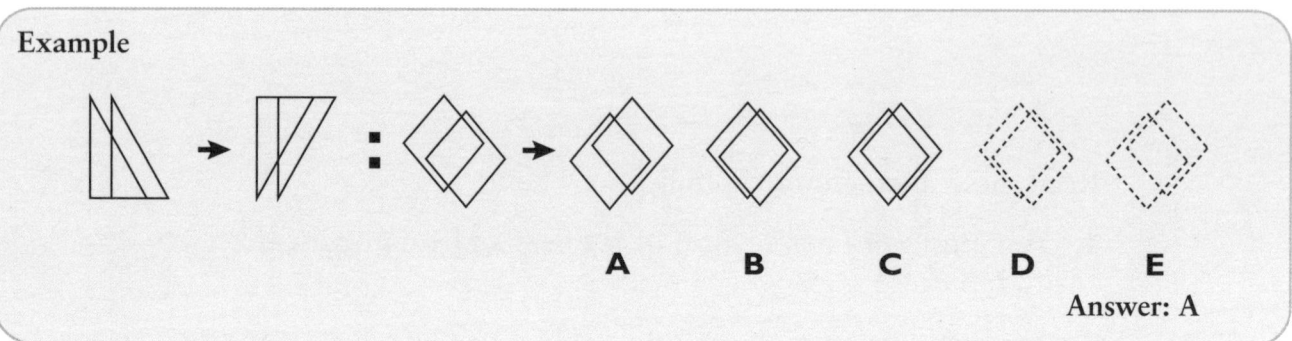

Answer: A

Now try these practice questions.

P1.

P2.

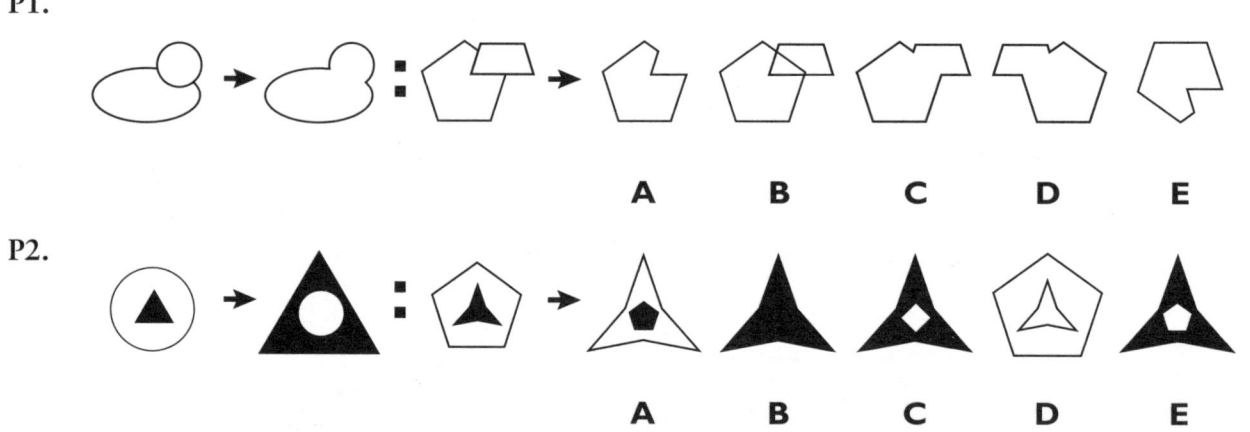

WAIT UNTIL YOU ARE TOLD TO GO ON

1.

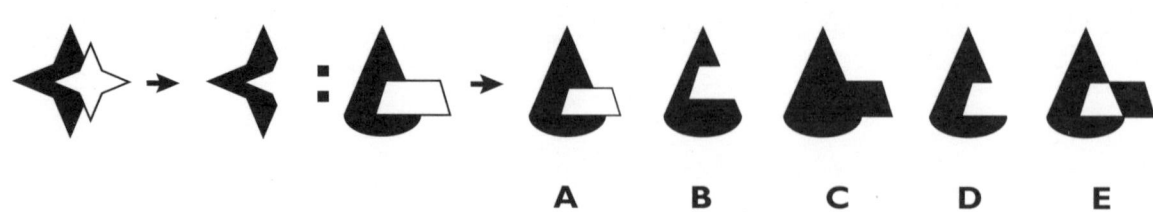

NOW GO ON TO THE NEXT PAGE

2.

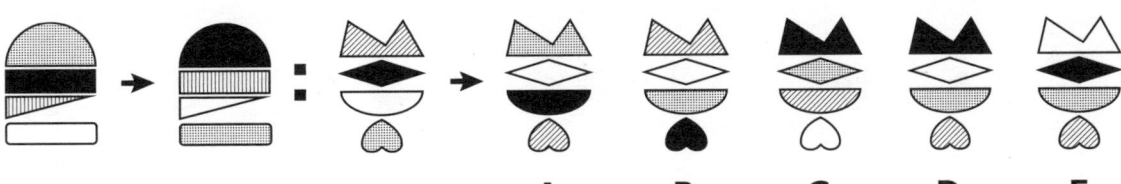

A B C D E

3.

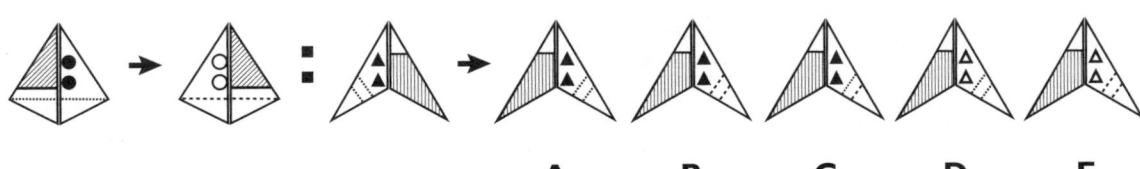

A B C D E

4.

A B C D E

5.

A B C D E

6.

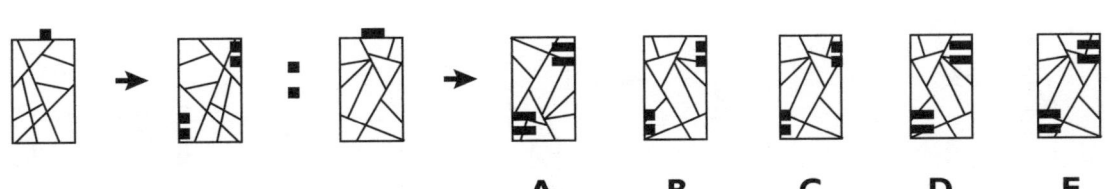

A B C D E

7.

A B C D E

NOW GO ON TO THE NEXT PAGE

8.

9.
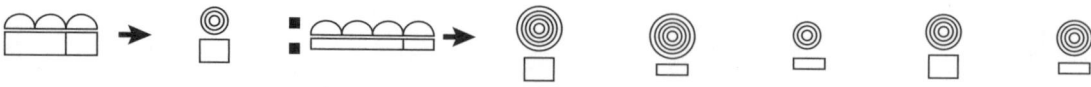

10.
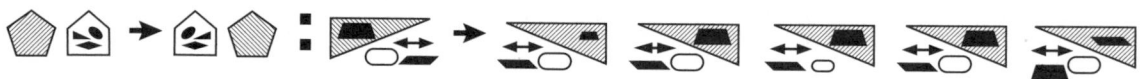

11.
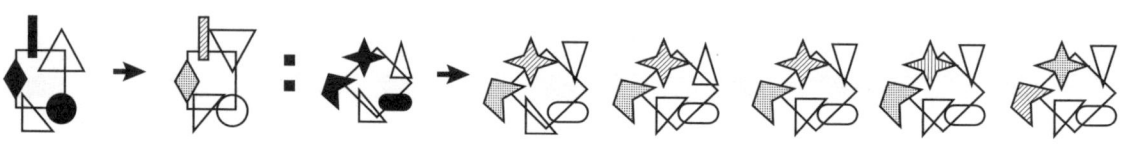

12.
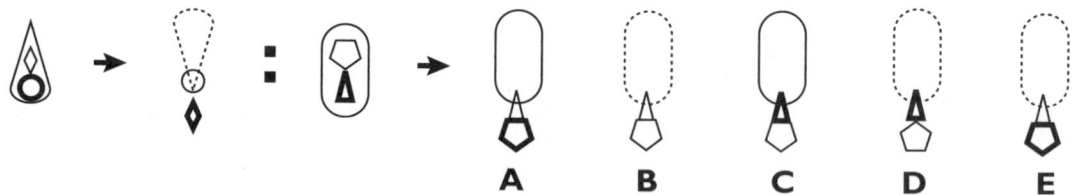

WAIT UNTIL YOU ARE TOLD TO GO ON

Section 2

The following questions are about finding the odd one out in a series of shapes or patterns. Find the odd one out and mark it on your answer sheet.

Here is an example to help you.

Example

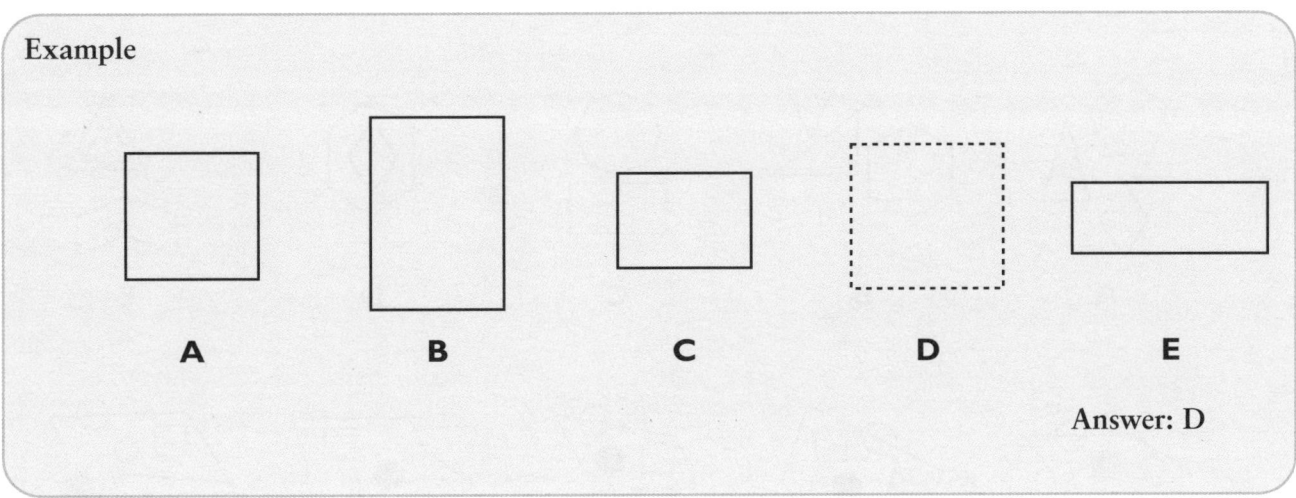

Answer: D

Now try these practice questions.

P1.

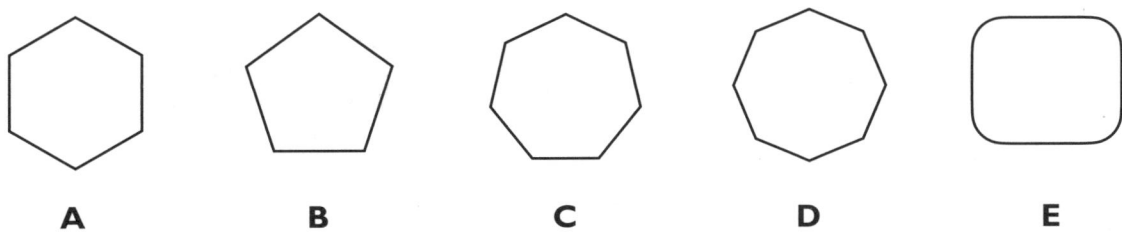

P2.

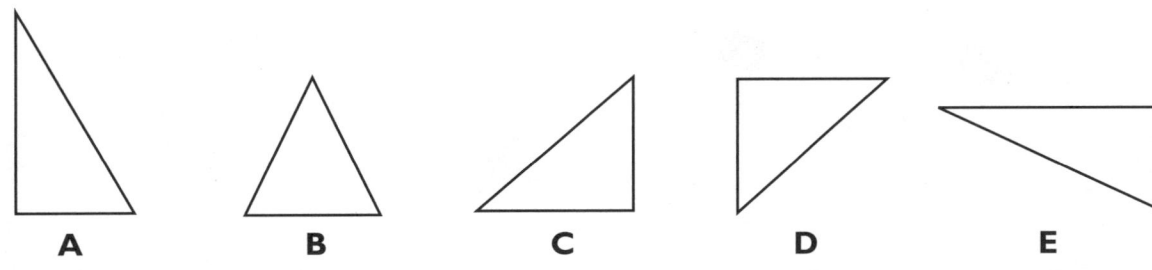

WAIT UNTIL YOU ARE TOLD TO GO ON

NOW GO ON TO THE NEXT PAGE

1.

A B C D E

2.

A B C D E

3.

A B C D E

4.

A B C D E

5.

A B C D E

6.

A B C D E

NOW GO ON TO THE NEXT PAGE

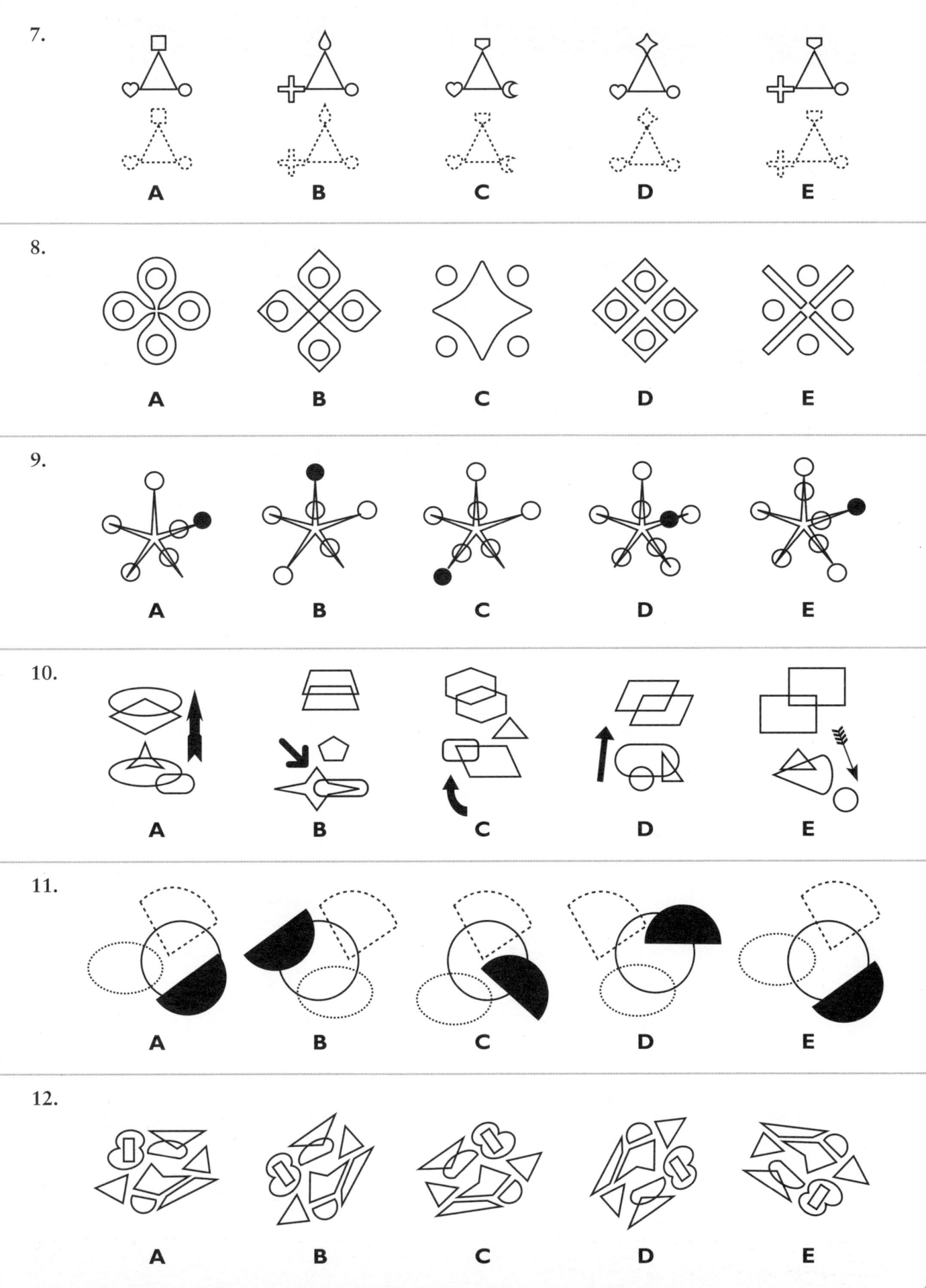

Section 3

In each question, use the faces given on the first two or three cubes to work out which face is labelled ? on the last cube. Choose one of the five options and mark it on your answer sheet.

Here is an example to help you.

Example

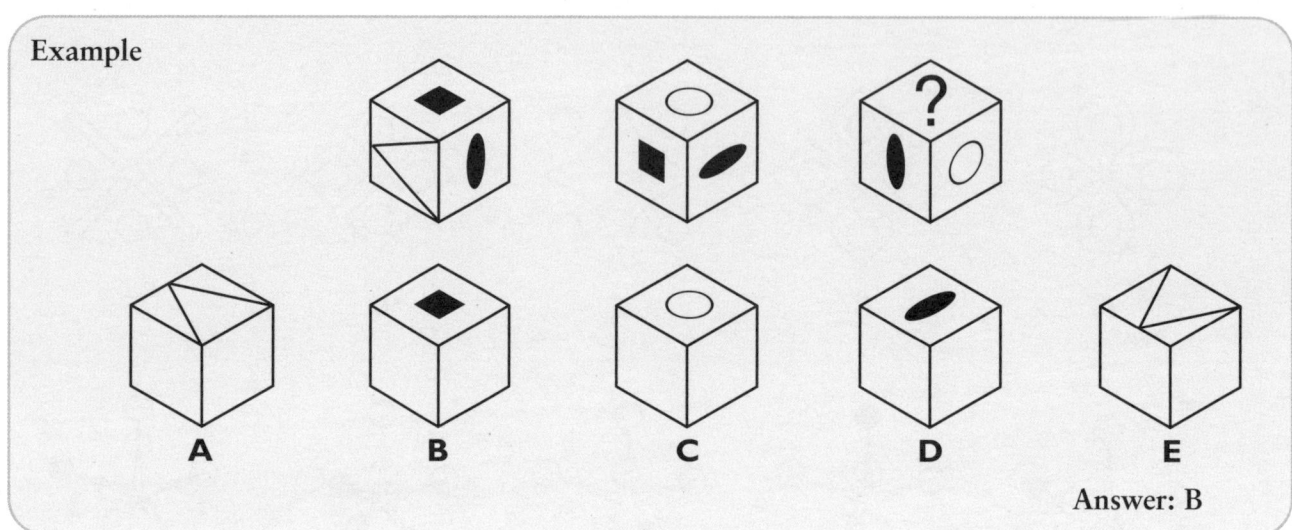

Answer: B

Now try these practice questions.

P1.

P2.

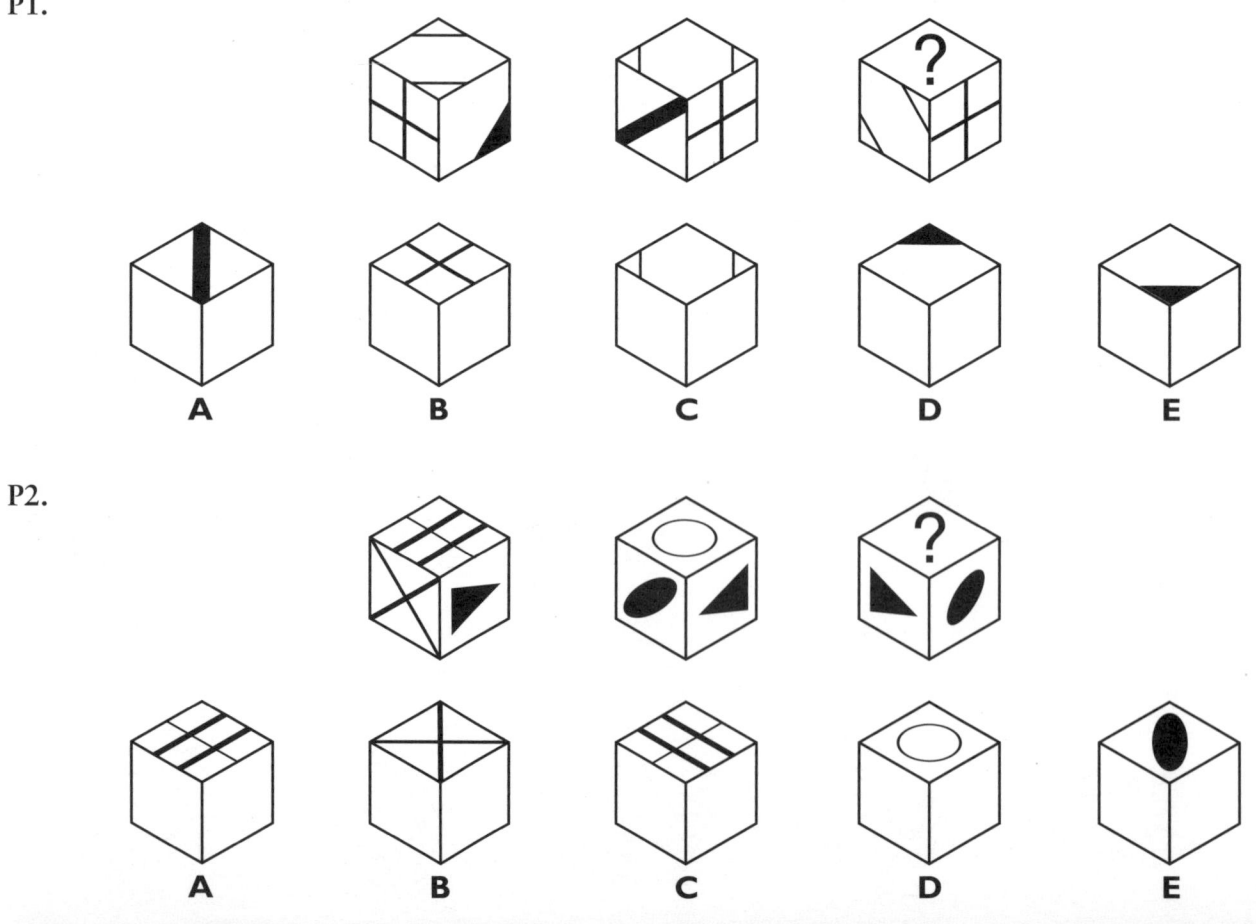

WAIT UNTIL YOU ARE TOLD TO GO ON

NOW GO ON TO THE NEXT PAGE

1.

2.

3.

4.

NOW GO ON TO THE NEXT PAGE

5.

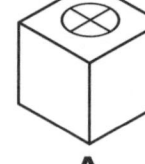 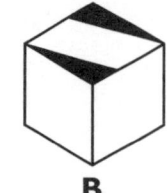 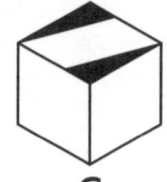 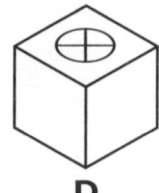 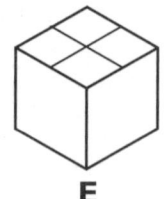

A　　　　B　　　　C　　　　D　　　　E

6.

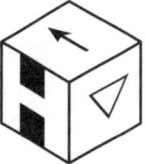 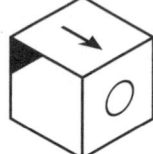 

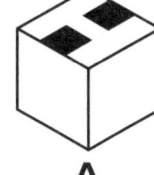 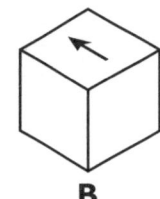 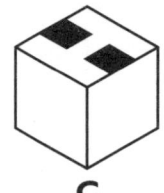 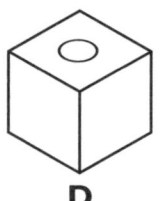 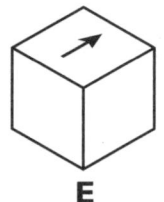

A　　　　B　　　　C　　　　D　　　　E

7.

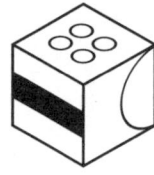 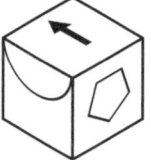 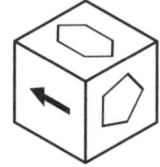 

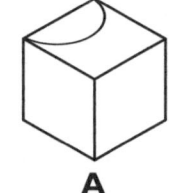  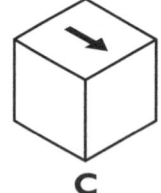 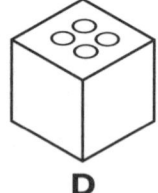 

A　　　　B　　　　C　　　　D　　　　E

8.

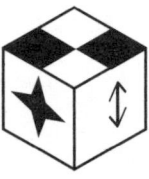 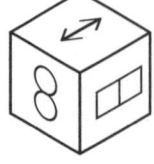  

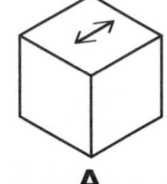 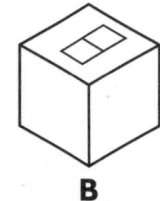 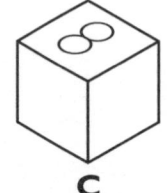 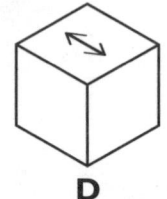 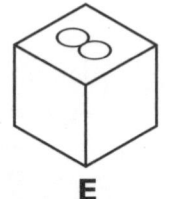

A　　　　B　　　　C　　　　D　　　　E

NOW GO ON TO THE NEXT PAGE

9.

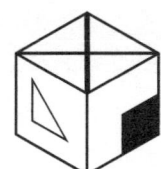   

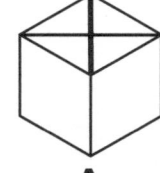 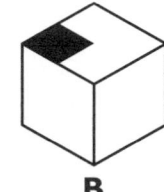 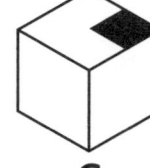 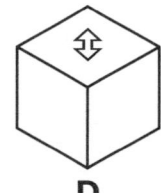 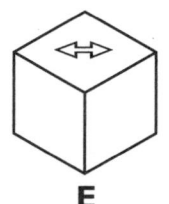

A   **B**   **C**   **D**   **E**

10.

 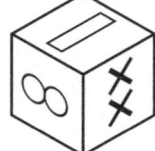 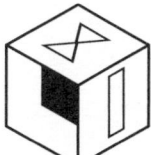 

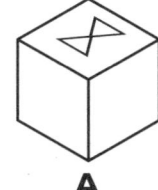 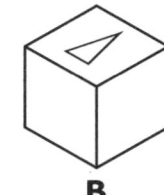 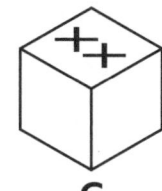 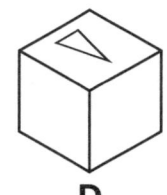 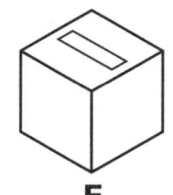

A   **B**   **C**   **D**   **E**

11.

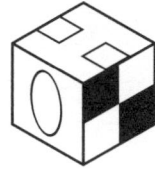  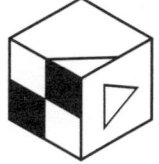 

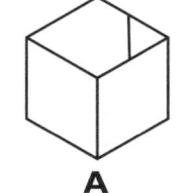 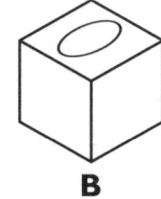 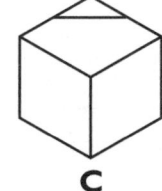 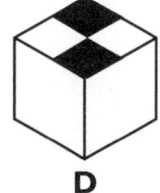 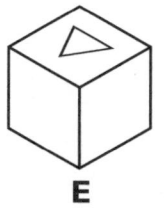

A   **B**   **C**   **D**   **E**

12.

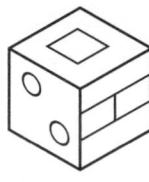   

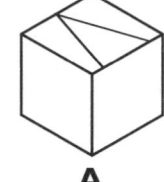 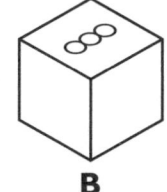 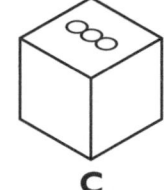 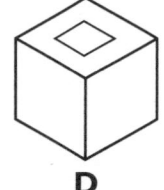 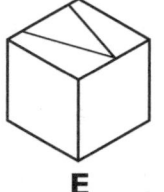

A   **B**   **C**   **D**   **E**

WAIT UNTIL YOU ARE TOLD TO GO ON

Section 4

In each question, the shape on the left is hidden in one of the figures on the right. It has not changed size and has not been rotated. Decide which figure contains the hidden shape and mark it on your answer sheet.

Here is an example to help you.

Example

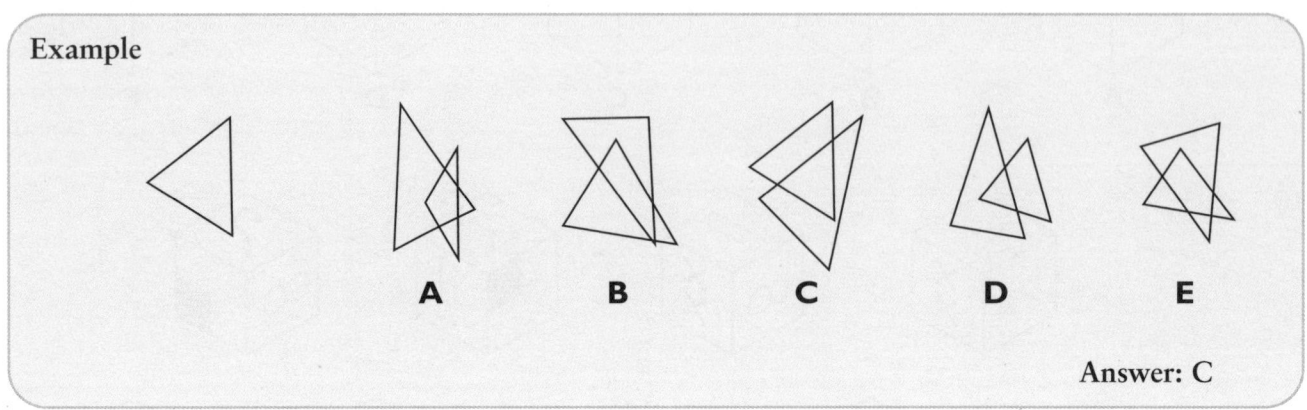

Answer: C

Now try these practice questions.

P1.

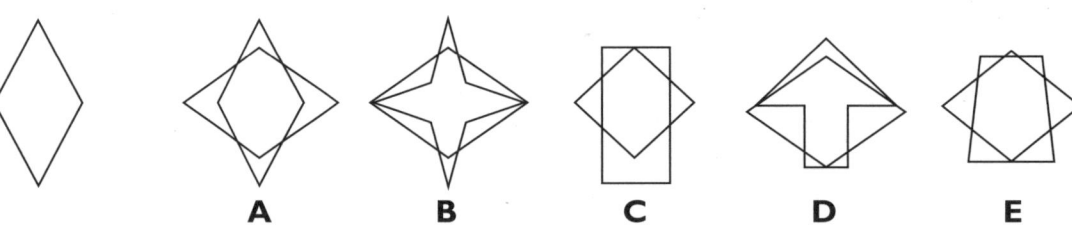

P2.

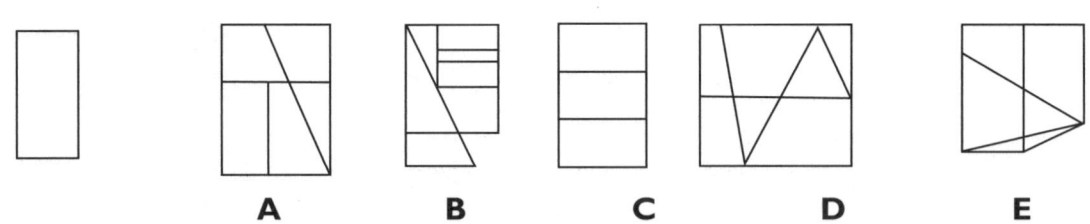

WAIT UNTIL YOU ARE TOLD TO GO ON

1.

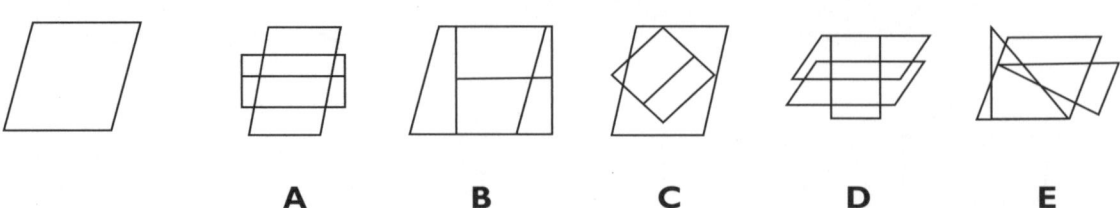

NOW GO ON TO THE NEXT PAGE

2.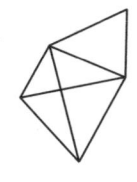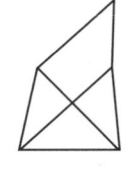
                   A   **B**   **C**   **D**   **E**

3.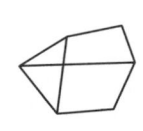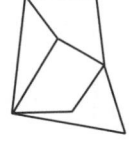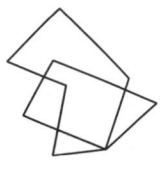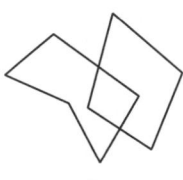
                   A   **B**   **C**   **D**   **E**

4.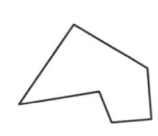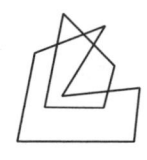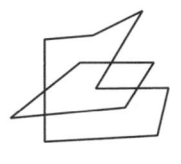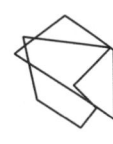
                   A   **B**   **C**   **D**   **E**

5.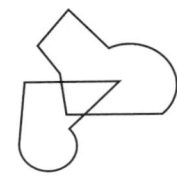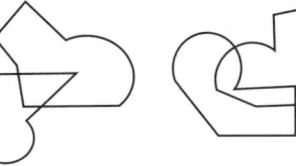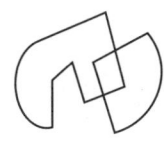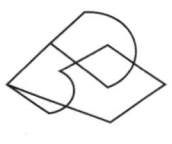
                   A   **B**   **C**   **D**   **E**

6.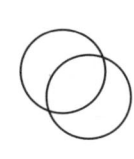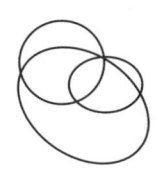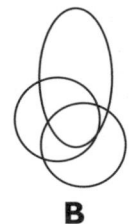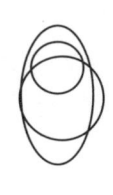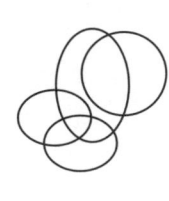
                   A   **B**   **C**   **D**   **E**

7.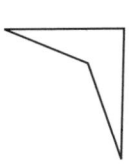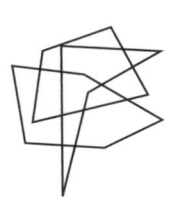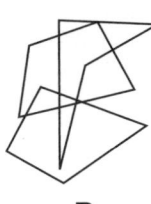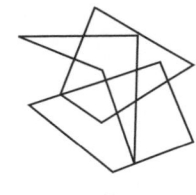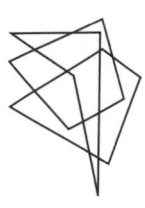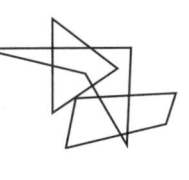
                   A   **B**   **C**   **D**   **E**

NOW GO ON TO THE NEXT PAGE

8.

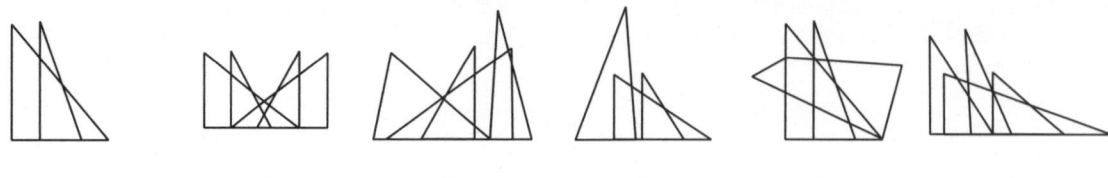

9.

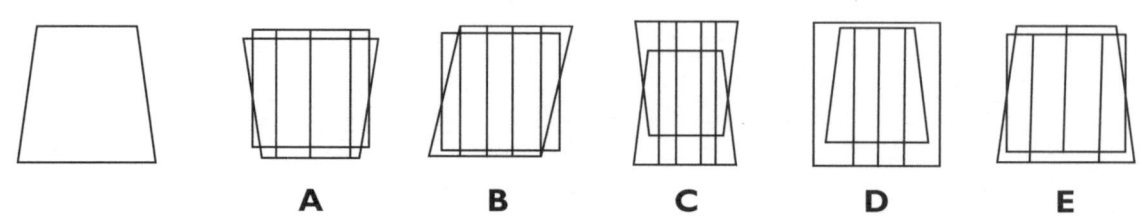

10.

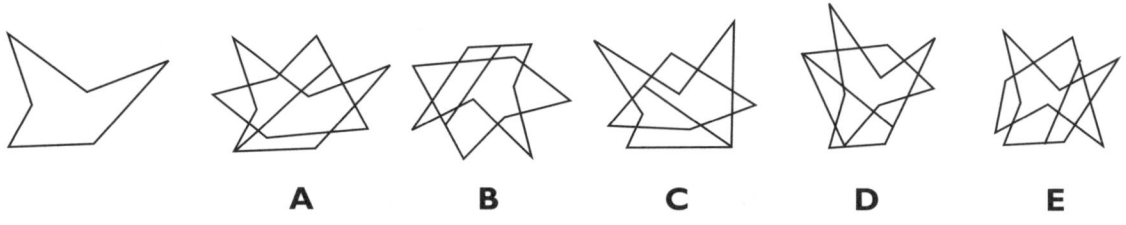

11.

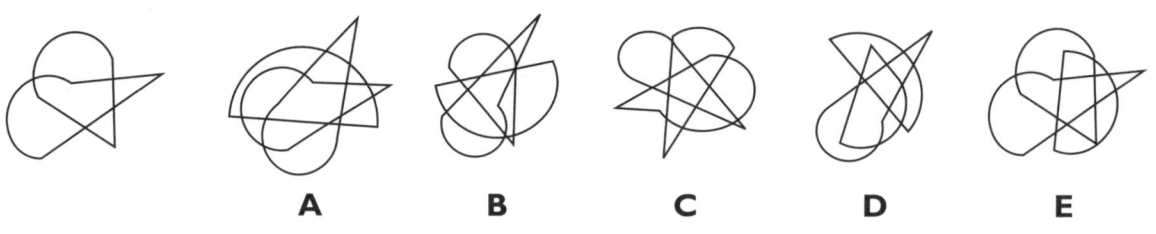

12.

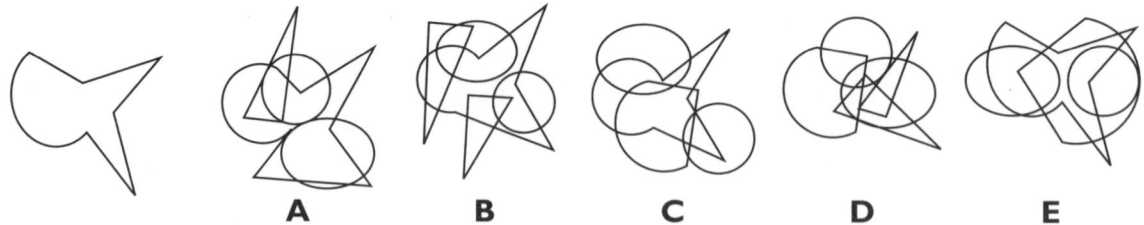

WAIT UNTIL YOU ARE TOLD TO GO ON

Section 5

In each question, the steps show a square of paper that is folded along the dashed lines and has some holes punched through. Decide which figure on the right shows what the paper will look like after it has been unfolded. Mark its letter on your answer sheet.

Here is an example to help you.

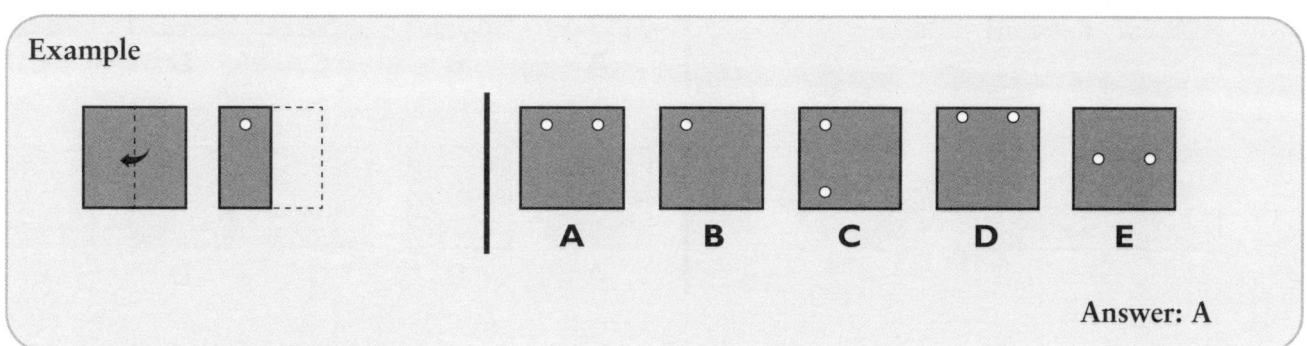

Answer: A

Now try these practice questions.

P1.

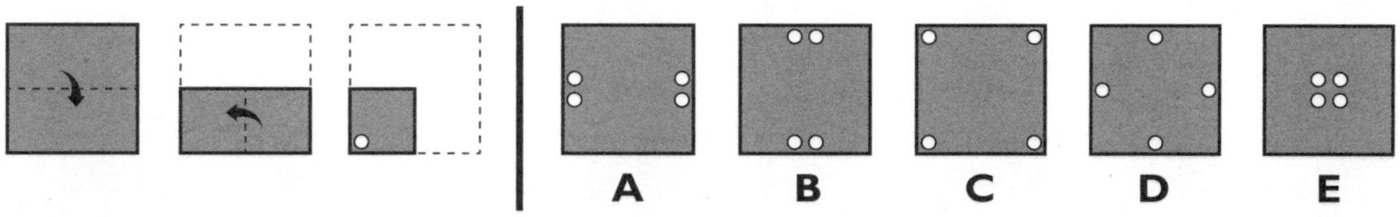

P2.

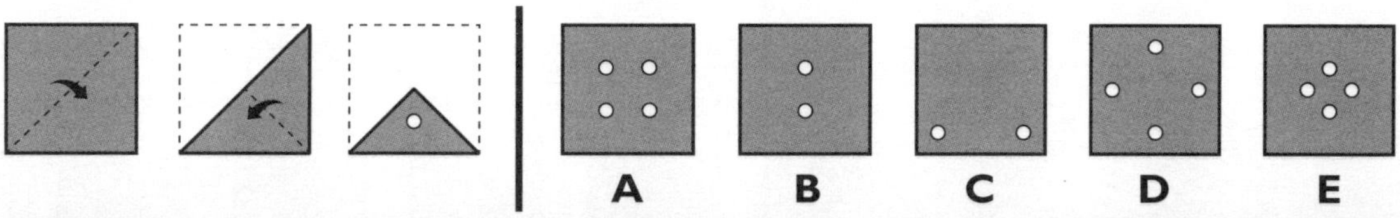

WAIT UNTIL YOU ARE TOLD TO GO ON

1.

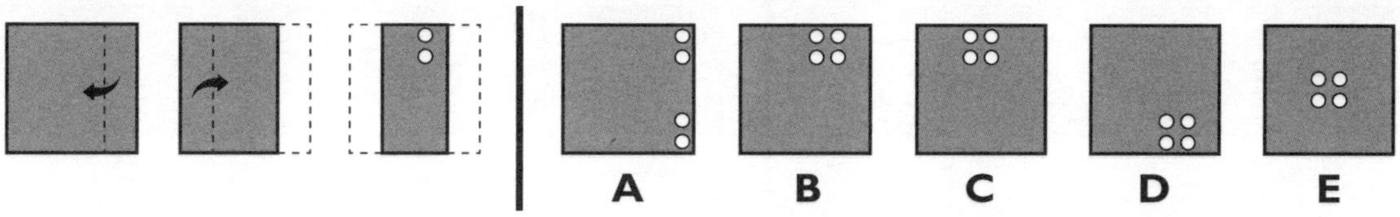

2.

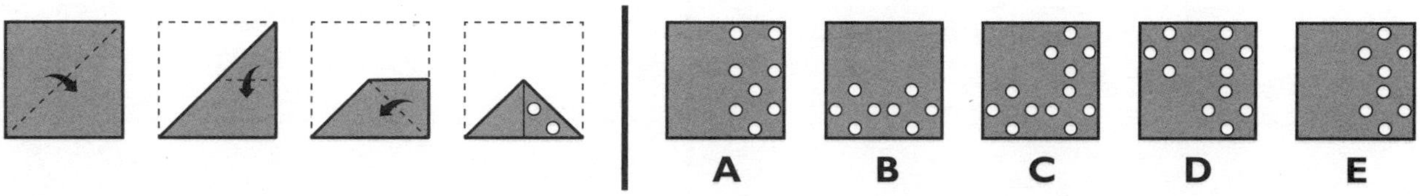

3.

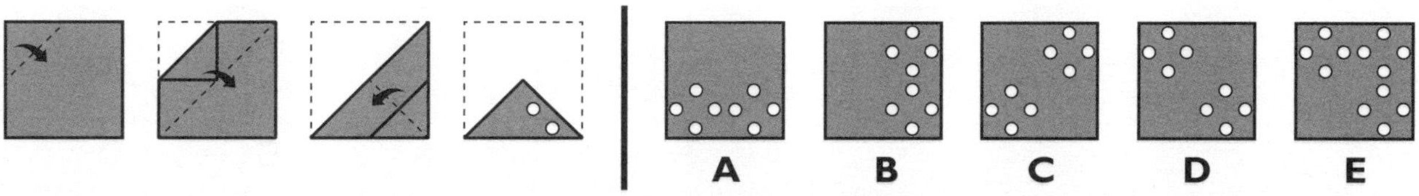

NOW GO ON TO THE NEXT PAGE

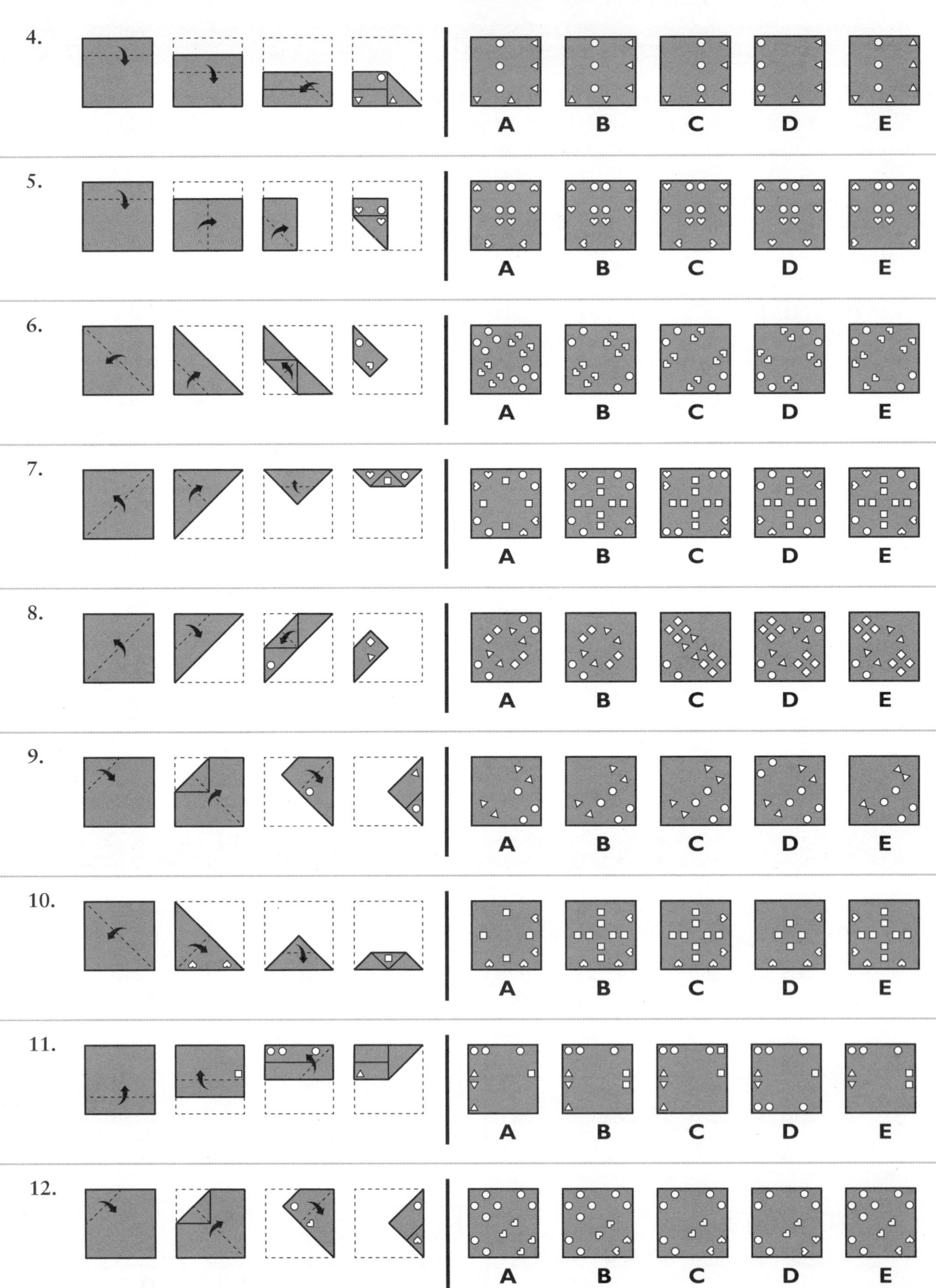

Non-Verbal Reasoning
Multiple-Choice
Practice Test D

Read these instructions carefully.

1. You must not open or turn over this booklet until you are told to do so.

2. The booklet contains a multiple-choice test, in which you have to mark your answer to each question on the separate answer sheet.

3. There are five sections in this test. Each section starts with an explanation of what to do, followed by an example. Explanations of the answers for these are included in the answer key. You will then be asked to do two practice questions.

4. You should indicate one answer only for each question by drawing a firm pencil line clearly through the rectangle next to your answer on the answer sheet. Rub out any mistakes as well as you can and put in your new answer.

5. Complete the questions as quickly and carefully as you can. If you find that you cannot do a question, do not waste time on it but go on to the next one.

6. You should do any rough working on a separate sheet of paper.

Section 1

In each question, there are five boxes arranged in a series. One of the boxes is empty. Decide which box on the right completes the series and mark its letter on your answer sheet.

Here is an example to help you.

Answer: E

Now try these practice questions.

P1.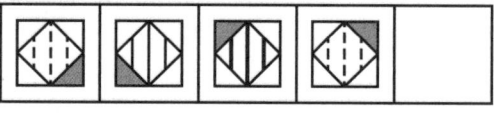
A B C D E

P2.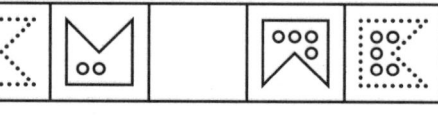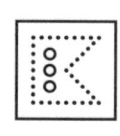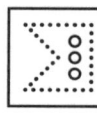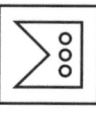
A B C D E

WAIT UNTIL YOU ARE TOLD TO GO ON

1.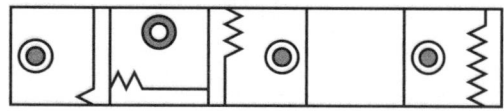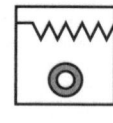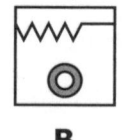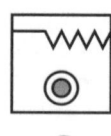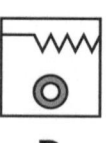
A B C D E

2.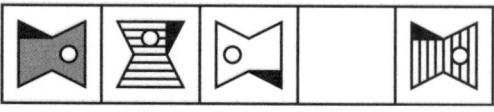
A B C D E

3.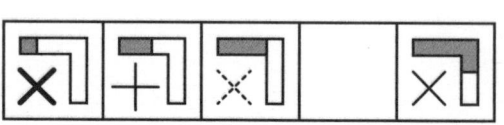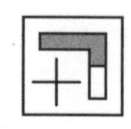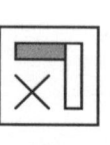
A B C D E

NOW GO ON TO THE NEXT PAGE

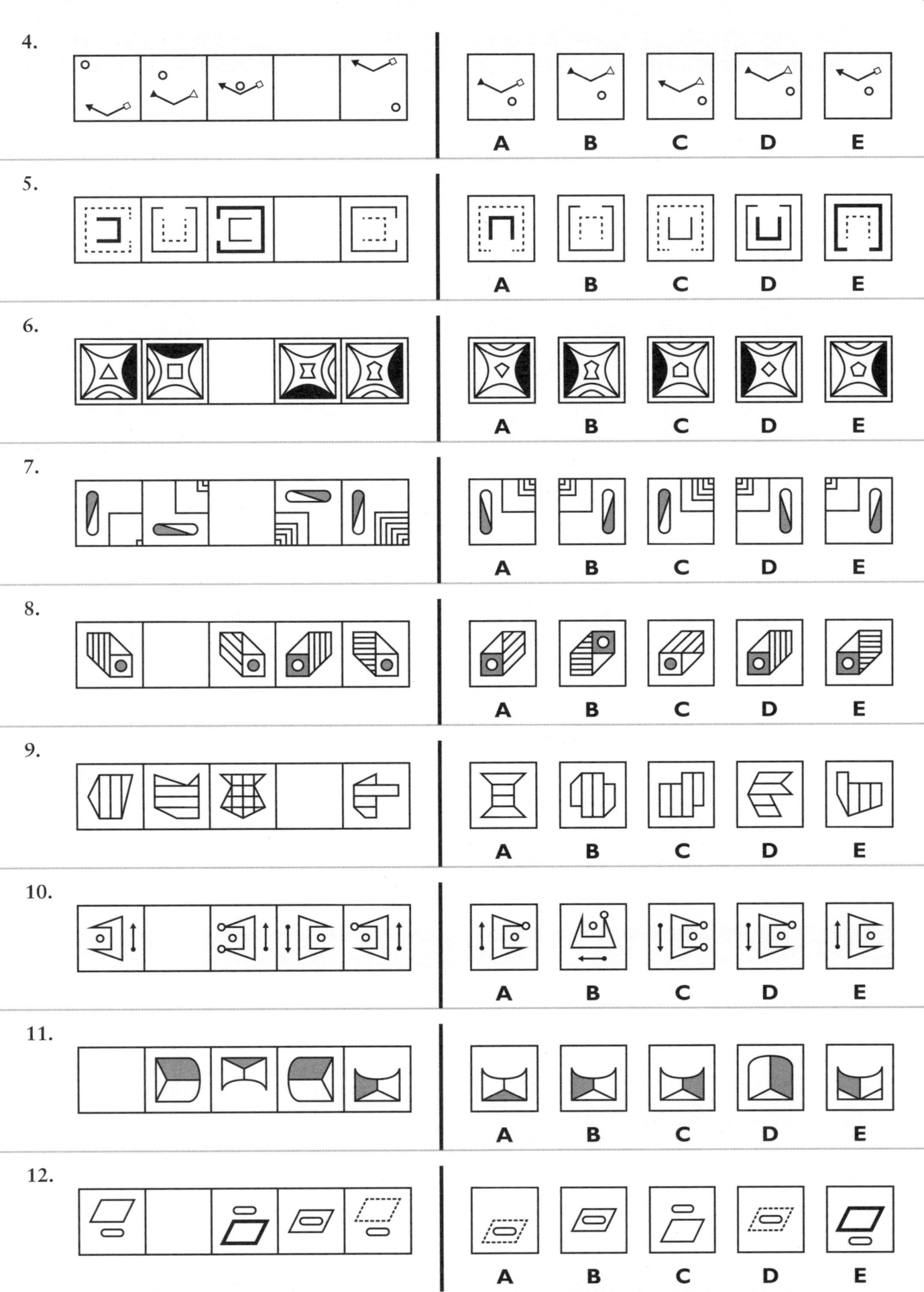

Section 2

In each question, three figures are shown on the left. They have something in common. Decide which of the options on the right is most like the figures on the left and mark its letter on your answer sheet.

Here is an example to help you.

Example

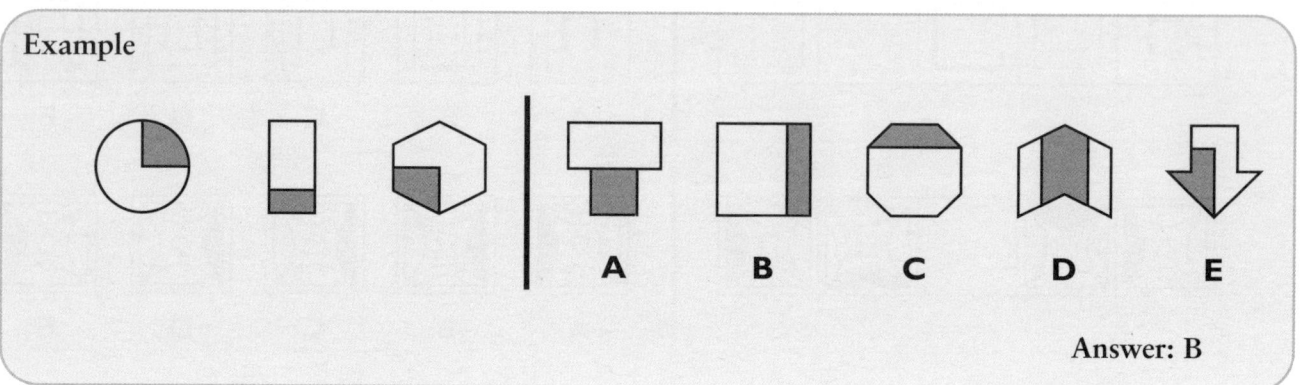

Answer: B

Now try these practice questions.

P1.

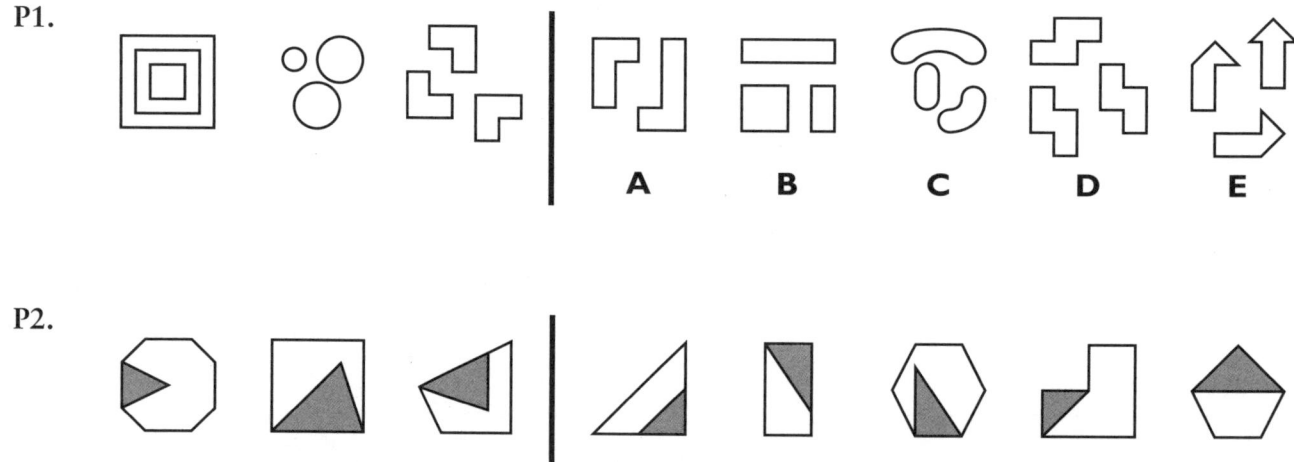

P2.

WAIT UNTIL YOU ARE TOLD TO GO ON

1.

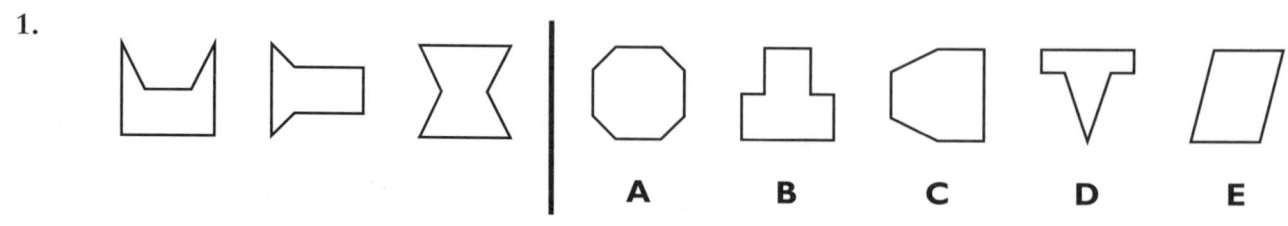

NOW GO ON TO THE NEXT PAGE

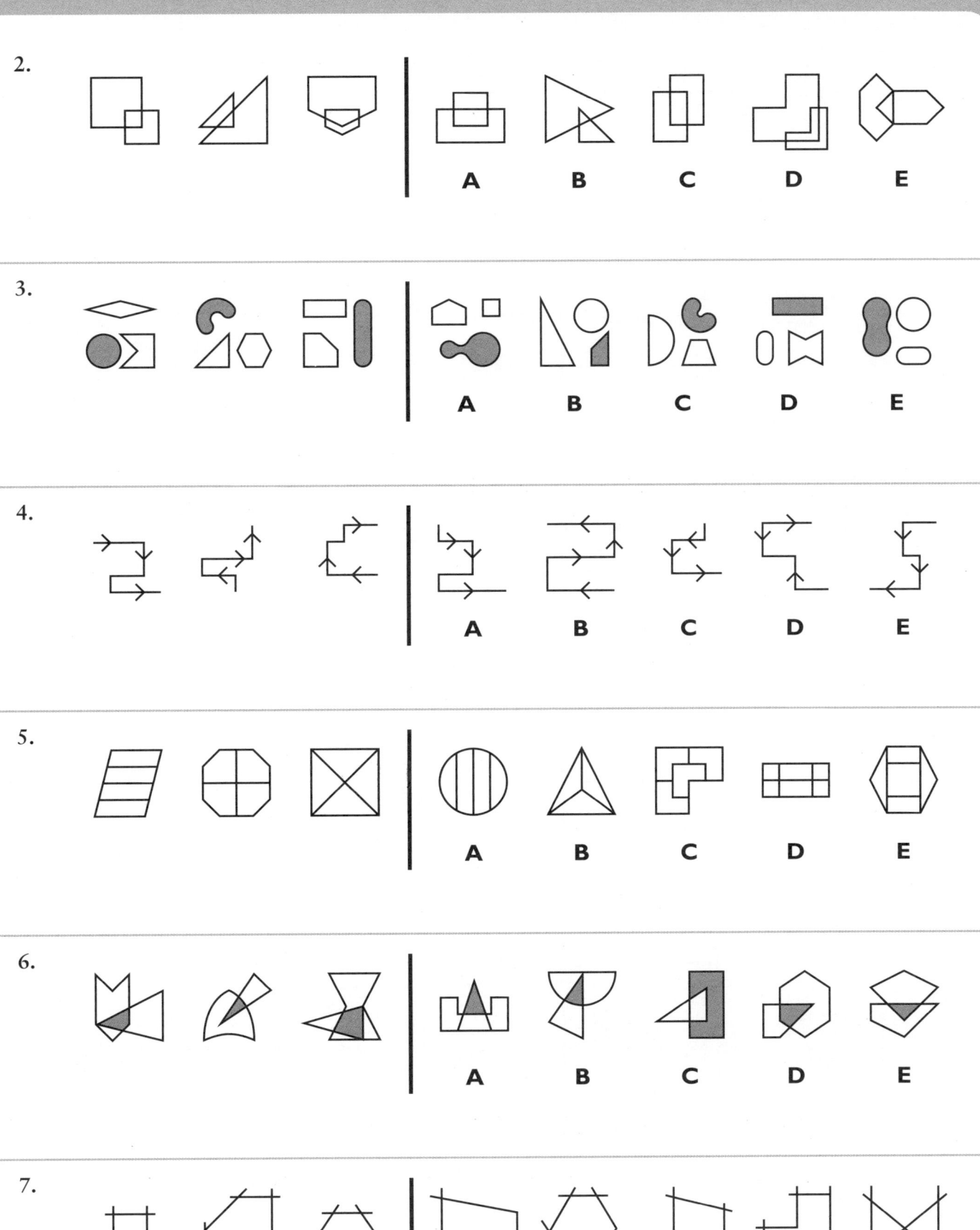

8.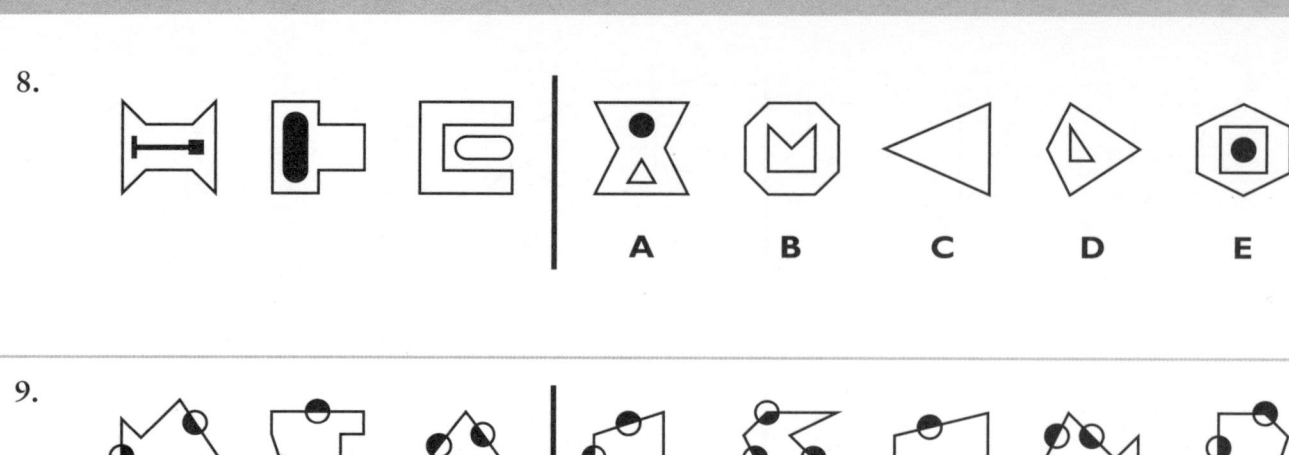

9.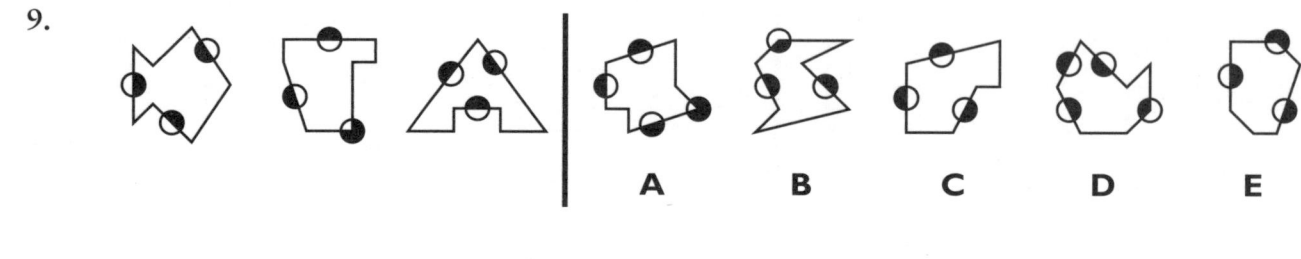

10.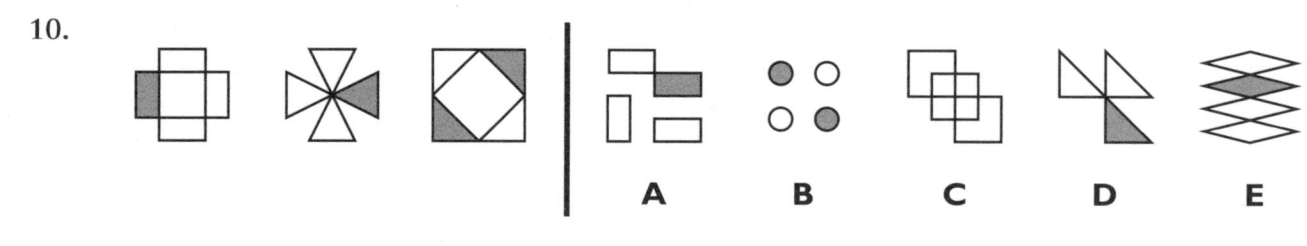

11.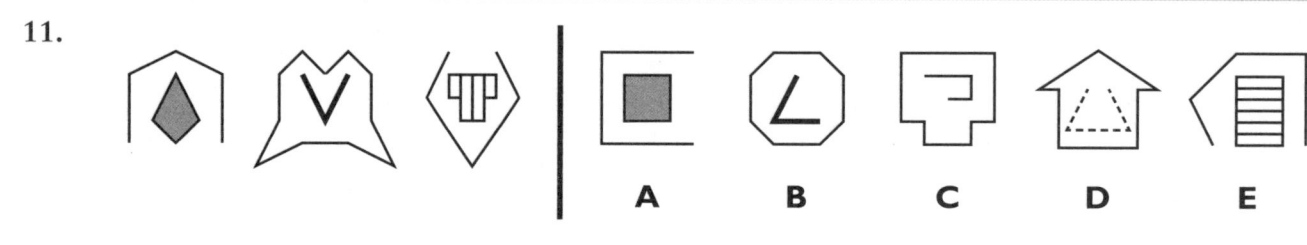

12.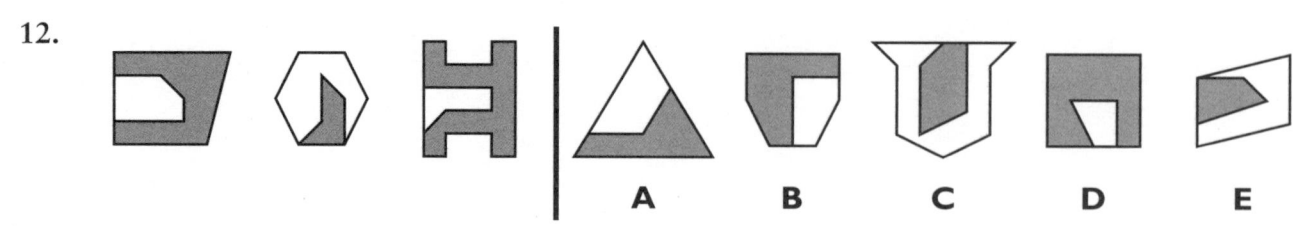

Section 3

The figures on the left each have a code. Work out how the codes go with these figures. Then look at the figure to the right of the vertical line and find its code from the options given. Mark its letter on your answer sheet.

Here is an example to help you.

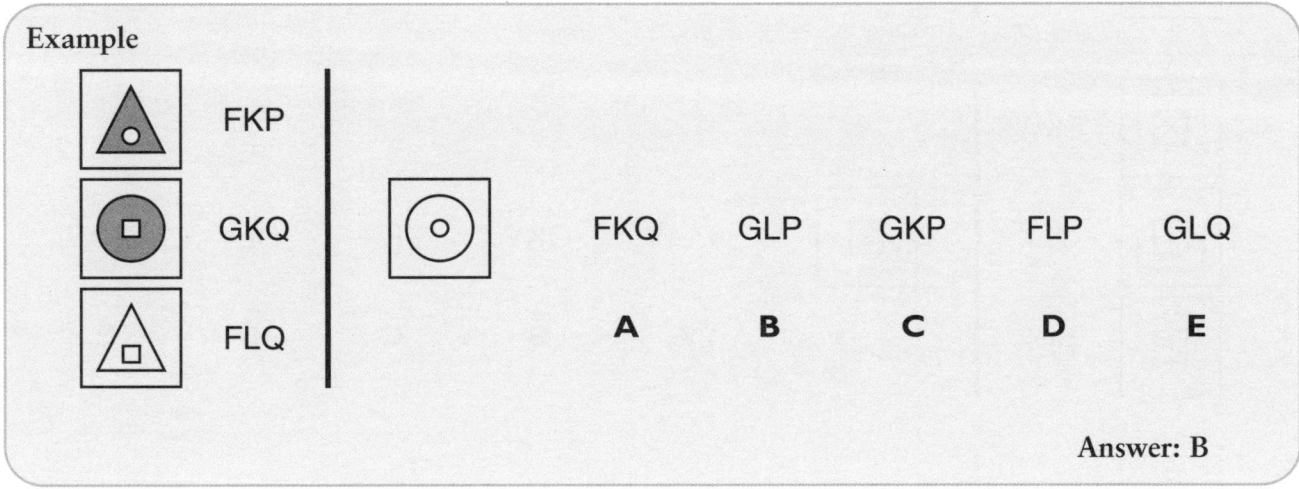

Answer: B

Now try these practice questions.

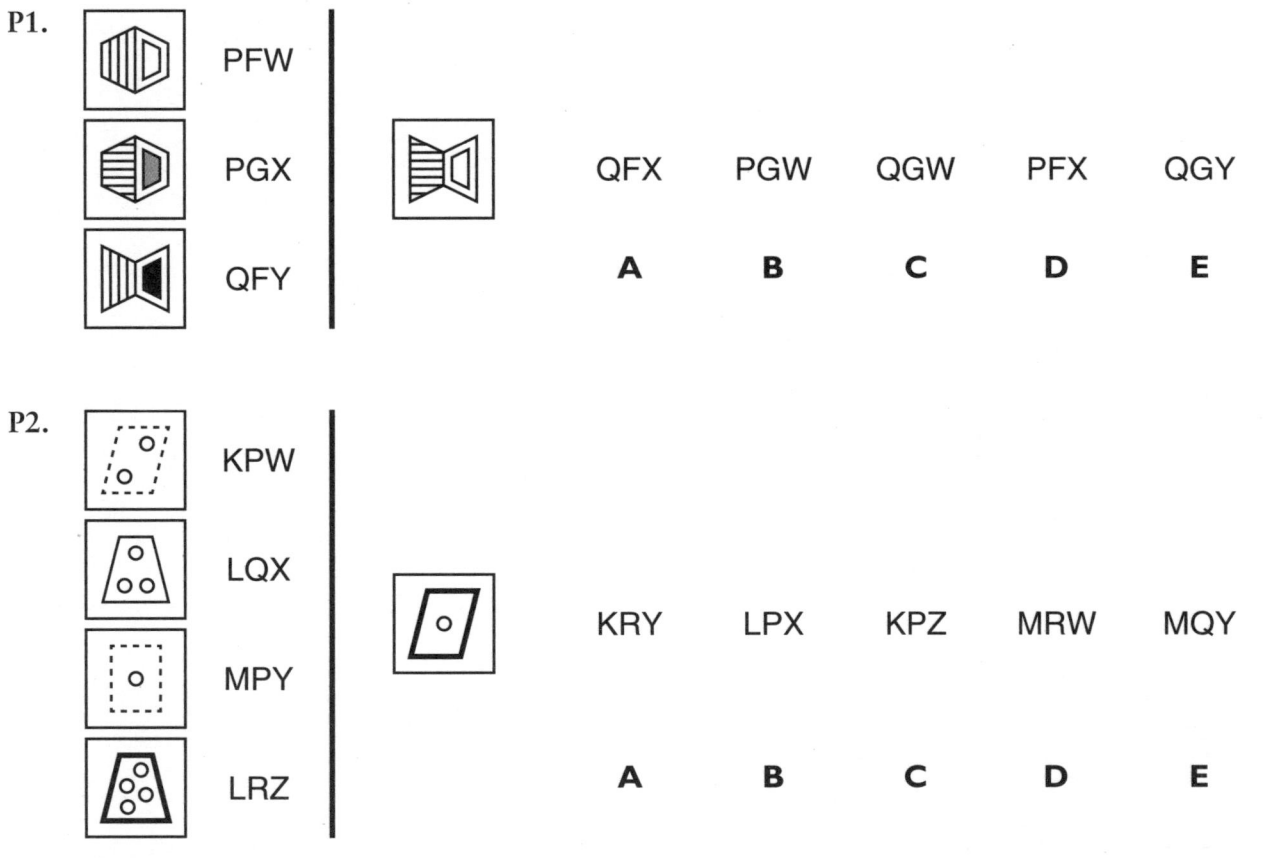

WAIT UNTIL YOU ARE TOLD TO GO ON

NOW GO ON TO THE NEXT PAGE

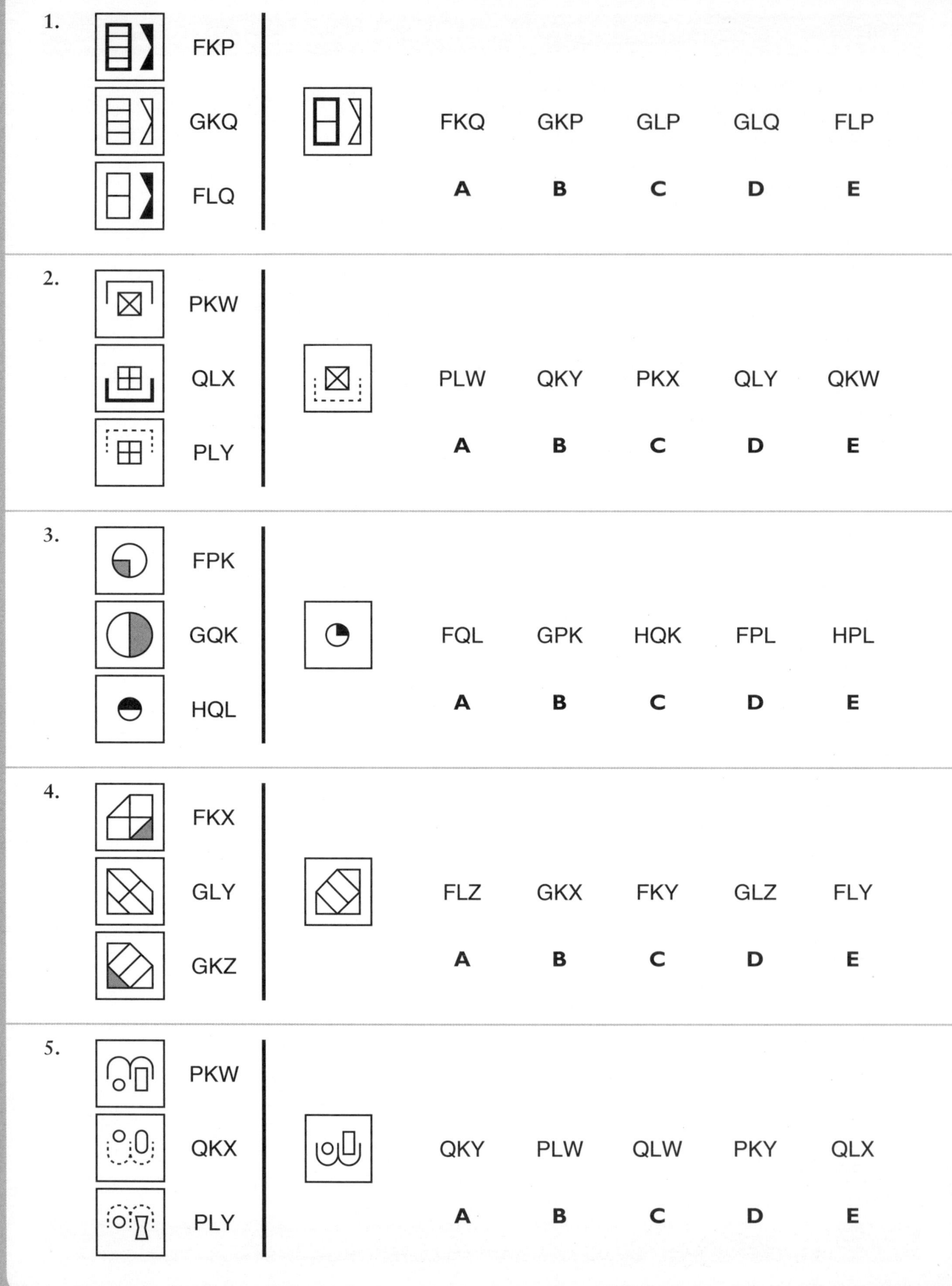

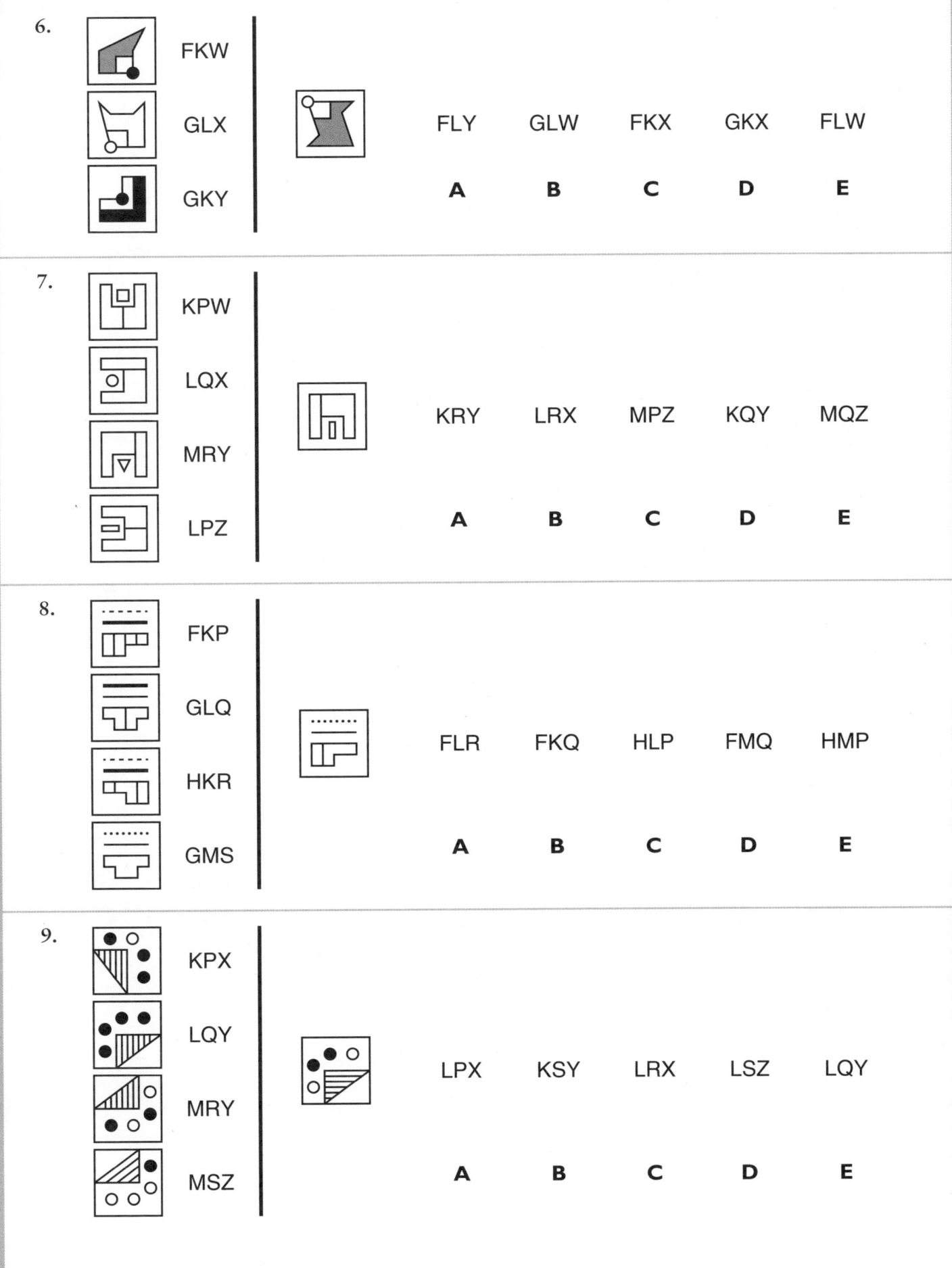

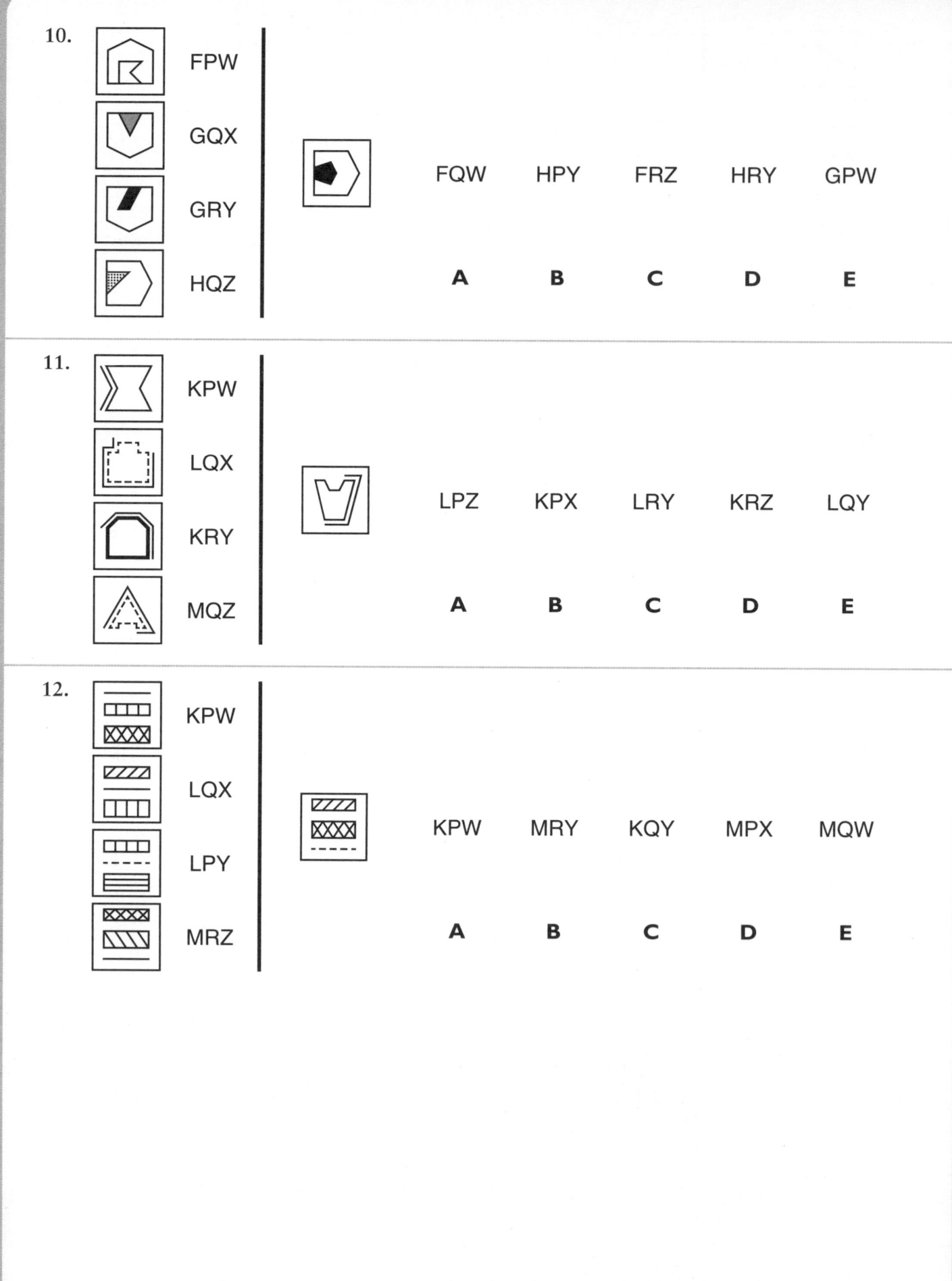

Section 4

In each question, one of the boxes in the grid is empty. Work out which one of the boxes on the right completes the grid and mark its letter on your answer sheet.

Here is an example to help you.

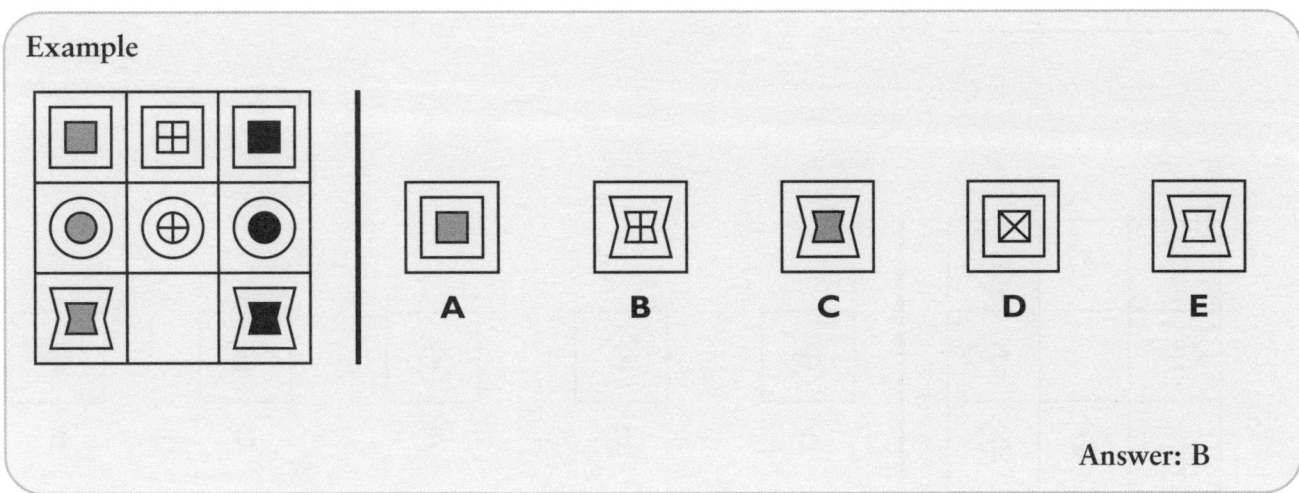

Answer: B

Now try these practice questions.

P1.

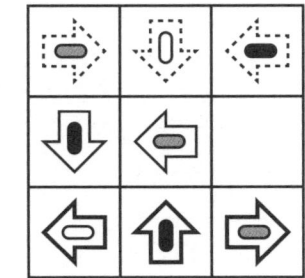   

A   B   C   D   E

P2.

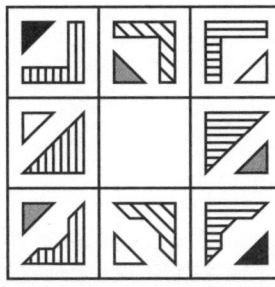     

A   B   C   D   E

WAIT UNTIL YOU ARE TOLD TO GO ON

NOW GO ON TO THE NEXT PAGE

1.

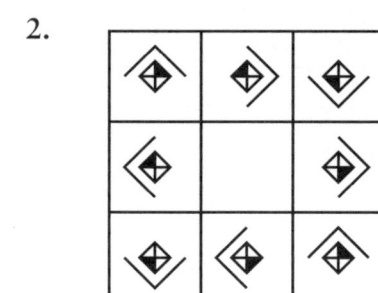
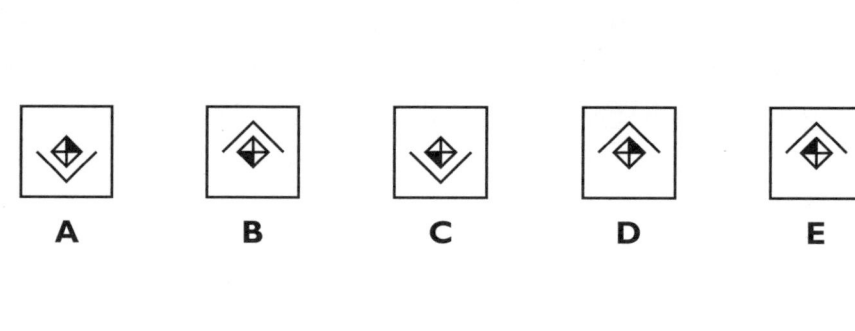

2.

3.

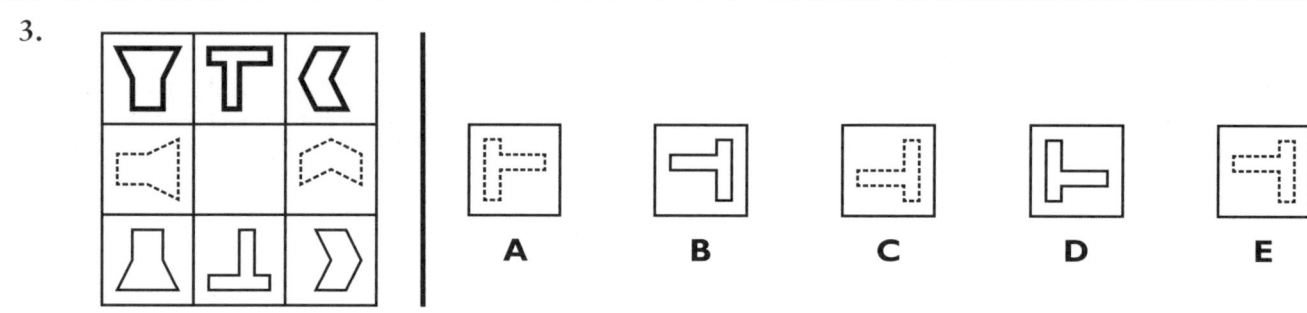

4.

NOW GO ON TO THE NEXT PAGE

5.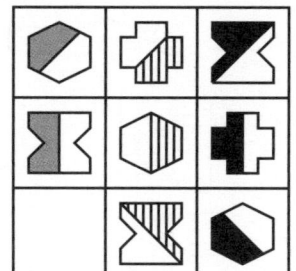

6.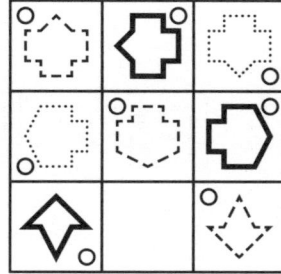

7.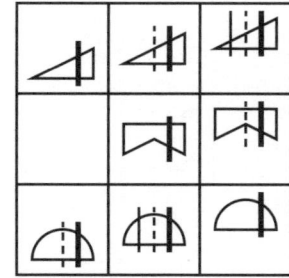

8.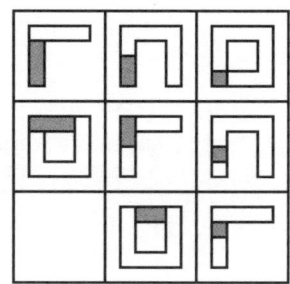

NOW GO ON TO THE NEXT PAGE

9.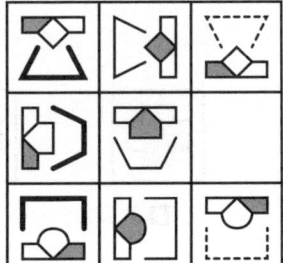

10.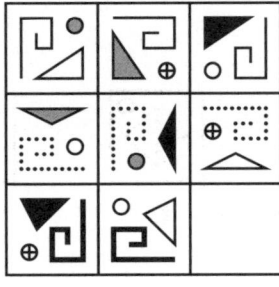

11.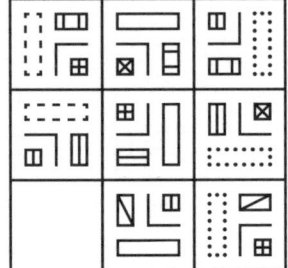

12.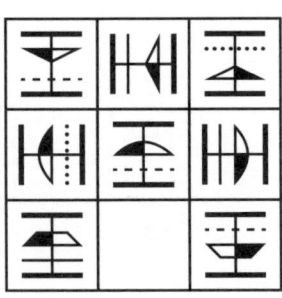

WAIT UNTIL YOU ARE TOLD TO GO ON

Section 5

In each question, look at the first figure on the left. It can be completed by the second figure plus one other figure from the options to the right. Find the correct figure on the right: it can be rotated but not reflected. Mark its letter on your answer sheet.

Here is an example to help you.

Example

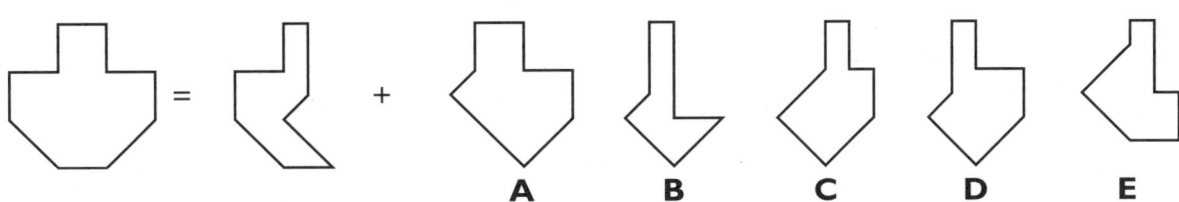

Answer: C

Now try these practice questions.

P1.

P2.

WAIT UNTIL YOU ARE TOLD TO GO ON

1.

2.

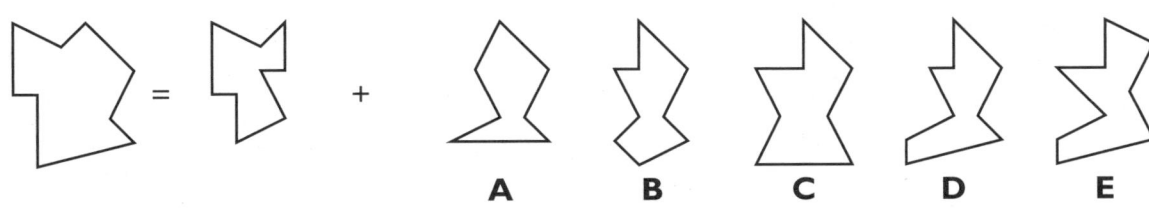

NOW GO ON TO THE NEXT PAGE

3.  = 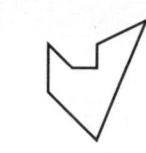 +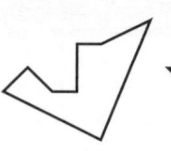

A B C D E

4. 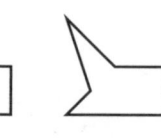 +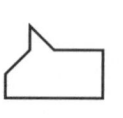

A B C D E

5.  +

A B C D E

6. 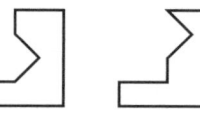 +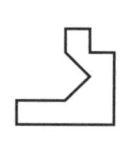

A B C D E

7.

A B C D E

8.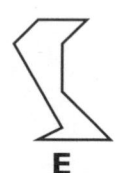

A B C D E

NOW GO ON TO THE NEXT PAGE

9.

10.

11.

12.

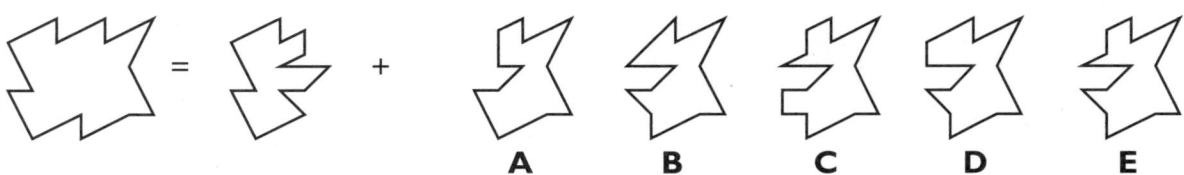

END OF TEST

TEST ADVICE

This information will not appear in the actual test.
It is included here to remind you not to stop working
until you are told the test is over.

CHECK YOUR ANSWERS AGAIN IF THERE IS TIME

CORRECTING EVEN ONE MISTAKE CAN MEAN AN EXTRA MARK

Collins
PRACTICE PAPERS

Answers and Explanations

Non-Verbal Reasoning

Marking

Award one mark for each correct answer. Half marks are not allowed, and marks are not given for 'very nearly correct answers'. No marks are deducted for wrong answers.

If scores are low, look at the paper and identify which question types seem to be harder for your child. Then spend some time going over them together. If your child is very accurate and gets correct answers, but works too slowly, try getting them to do one of the practice papers with time targets going through. If you are helpful and look for ways to help your child, they will grow in confidence and feel well prepared when they take the actual examinations.

Practice Test A Answers and Explanations

Section 1
E.g. A
P1. A
P2. C
1. A
2. D
3. A
4. E
5. E
6. D
7. E
8. C
9. B
10. A
11. D
12. B

Section 2
E.g. D
   Moving from left to right across the grid, the figure changes from black to no shading with a solid outline.
P1. A
   Moving from left to right across the grid, the polygon gains one additional side. The outline does not change.
P2. C
   Moving from left to right across the grid, the figures are reflected in a vertical mirror line.
1. C
   Moving from left to right across the grid, the figures are reflected in a vertical mirror line. Looking diagonally across the grid, the line type is consistent.
2. B
   Moving from top to bottom across the grid, the figures' positions are reflected in a horizontal mirror line. The figures themselves are not reflected, but the dashed outline becomes heavy and solid.
3. D
   Moving from left to right across the grid, each bracket style moves one place upwards.
4. E
   Moving from left to right across the grid, each figure is reflected in a vertical mirror line.
5. A
   Moving from left to right across the grid, solid and dashed lines are swapped for one another. The shading of the three small shapes is swapped between white and black. The small white shape does not change, but the small pentagon loses a side and becomes a small square, and the small hexagon gains a side and becomes a small heptagon.

6. B
   Moving from left to right across the grid, the upper shape is stretched horizontally, and the lower shape is raised to overlap with it. The lower shape is reflected in a horizontal mirror line.
7. A
   Moving from left to right across the grid, the outer and middle shapes swap places and sizes, and the inner circle changes into a triangle. The shading of the outer, middle and inner shapes does not change.
8. C
   Moving from left to right across the grid, the central shape rotates 180 degrees and the central dividing line rotates 90 degrees; the position of the four triangles moves one side clockwise. In each of the sections in the grid, the four black small squares are located closest to the centre of the grid.
9. E
   Moving from left to right across the grid, the striped rectangle becomes black and moves to the bottom right-hand side of each figure. Only the overlapping section of the larger shapes remains, also shaded black.
10. A
    Moving from left to right across the grid, each figure moves one place clockwise, and each style of shading and line type moves one place anticlockwise.
11. A
    Moving anticlockwise around the grid, the long arrow with the black arrowhead is rotated 90 degrees anticlockwise. The bold line with the white square alternates sides in each figure in the grid, and the line with the black dot alternates sides in each figure in the grid.
12. E
    Moving from left to right across the grid, the direction of the curved arrow changes from clockwise to anticlockwise and the arrowhead changes from open to solid black. The large shape gains an additional side. The placement of the double short perpendicular lines and the single short perpendicular line swaps.

Section 3
E.g. A
   Moving from left to right, the figure has been reflected in a horizontal mirror line.
P1. C
   Moving from left to right, the overlapping figures are changed to simply an outline.
P2. E
   Moving from left to right, the two figures swap position and size, but the shading of each figure does not change.

1. **B**
   Moving from left to right, the figure is reflected in a horizontal mirror line.
2. **E**
   Moving from left to right, the black-shaded shape changes to white shading and gains a dashed outline. The white-shaded shape with a solid outline does not change.
3. **B**
   Moving from left to right, the shield shape becomes smaller, shaded black and then doubled. The small shields are arranged vertically inside the larger shape and rotated 180 degrees. Behind both, a curve-ended rectangle is added that overlaps with the larger shape from the left-hand side of the question.
4. **A**
   Moving from left to right, the first figure shown is doubled, with the additional figure being added above the original. The additional figure is reflected in a horizontal mirror line before being added. The small black shapes then move towards one another so they slightly overlap.
5. **E**
   The initial figure is composed of two white figures, one longer than the other, and two smaller black figures, one of which is larger than the other. Moving from left to right, the smaller black figure is enlarged and encapsulates all the other figures. The larger black figure loses its shading and moves to the same position that the smaller black figure had occupied. The entire figure is rotated 90 degrees anticlockwise.
6. **B**
   Moving from left to right, the figure is made smaller and reflected in a vertical mirror line. A diagonal line runs from bottom left to top right through the figure. A small, black-shaded figure is added at the bottom end of the diagonal line. This additional, black-shaded figure has one more side than the polygons making up the original figure.
7. **C**
   Moving from left to right, the horizontal line at the base of the figure becomes dashed. The whole figure is rotated 90 degrees clockwise. The shading of the small figures swaps from black to white and vice-versa.
8. **A**
   Moving from left to right, the solid lines take on the same line type as the lines with small circles at either end. The arrowheads change from open to black-shaded, and the small circles change to small squares. The whole figure gains a circle around the outside.
9. **C**
   Moving from left to right, the small striped figure is enlarged, and the upper small white figure is shaded black, doubled and placed inside. The lower white figure gains another, smaller version inside, which then overlaps the outside of the largest figure. The black figure disappears completely. The concentric white figures are positioned to the opposite side they appear on in the left-hand side of the question.
10. **A**
    Moving from left to right, the small endpoints on the left-hand arrows in the figure are enlarged. The uppermost endpoint gives the shape for the largest figure on the right-hand side of the question, which takes on a solid outline. The lowest endpoint gives the shape for the middle figure on the right-hand side of the question, which takes on a dashed outline. The two small shapes inside the figure swap shading, and are arranged inside one another, with the upper shape becoming the larger of the two.
11. **E**
    Moving from left to right, the striped figure is enlarged. The small, black-shaded figure gains the same shading and is replicated as many times as there were sides on the original outer shape. The arrow is replicated and merged into the outside of the large shape. It does not change direction.
12. **D**
    Moving from left to right, the figure is rotated 90 degrees anticlockwise. The small shape which appears in the centre of the overall figure remains the same. The small shape in the black outer triangle is replicated in the white outer triangle, and the small shape in the black outer square is replicated in the white outer square.

Section 4
E.g. C
P1. A
P2. E
1. B
2. D
3. E
4. C
5. C
6. A
7. A
8. B
9. B
10. B
11. E
12. A

Section 5
E.g. **D**
All of the figures have solid lines except for option D, which has dashed lines.
P1. **E**
All of the figures have pointed corners except for option E, which has curved corners.
P2. **B**
All of the other triangles have a right angle.
1. **E**
   In all the other figures, the smaller shape is positioned to the inside left of the larger shape.
2. **B**
   In all the other figures, the triangle overlaps with the oval with a single corner rather than two.
3. **C**
   In all the other figures, the black dots are arranged with two on the sides of the double arrowhead and two on the corners of the double arrowhead.
4. **D**
   In all the other figures, the arrow points to a white shape.
5. **E**
   In all the other figures, moving from the outer shape towards the inner shape, the number of sides of the shape decreases by one each time.
6. **D**
   In all the other figures, the dashed lines are parallel with one another.
7. **B**
   In all the other figures, the diagonal lines in the small square run from bottom left to top right.
8. **E**
   In all the other figures, the dashed oval is transparent rather than solid white.
9. **A**
   All of the other figures are rotations of one another, whereas A is a mirror image of the others.
10. **C**
    In all the other figures, the white polygons have consecutive numbers of sides. The black shapes (which are the same shape as the overlaps) are distractors.
11. **D**
    In all the other figures, the curved-ended rectangle points towards the circle rather than the triangle.
12. **E**
    In all the other figures, the small black triangle is not equilateral.

Practice Test B Answers and Explanations

Section 1
E.g. E WL
P = black shading, W = no shading
N = right-angled triangle, L = equilateral triangle

P1. B ZB
Y = white star, Z = black star
A = star at top of figure, B = star at bottom

P2. C UX
R = pentagon, S = hexagon, T = octagon, U = heptagon
V = small polygon, W = medium polygon, X = large polygon

1. **C MK**
   N = black shape is horizontal, M = black shape is vertical
   J = white shape is on top of the black shape, K = white shape is behind the black shape

2. **E JP**
   Q = black pentagon, J = black hexagon, V = black quadrilateral
   O = short dashes making up the diagonal line, P = long dashes making up the diagonal line, R = dots making up the diagonal line, S = solid diagonal line

3. **D DN**
   A = striped shading at top right, B = striped shading at top left, C = striped shading at bottom left, D = striped shading at bottom right
   M = star at bottom left, N = star at top right

4. **E FH**
   F = striped shading at top left, E = striped shading at bottom left, G = striped shading on right-hand side
   H = small, curved-cornered square at bottom of figure, I = small oval at bottom of figure

5. **A WB**
   T = long dashes in the dividing line, N = short dashes in the dividing line, W = solid dividing line, Z = dots in the dividing line
   A = dividing line is central in the octagon, B = dividing line is to the left of the octagon, Y = dividing line is to the right of the octagon

6. **E TS**
   E = arrow with four notches at one end, F = arrow with square at one end, T = arrow with hexagon at one end
   H = arrow points to the bottom right, G = arrow points to the bottom left, S = arrow points to the top left, U = arrow points to the top right

7. **C JW**
   J = endpoints are different, M = endpoints are the same
   P = solid line, W = dashed line, Q = dotted line

8. **C WT**
   V, W, X, Y = each letter refers to the specific type of curve
   T = curves are reflections of one another, with a vertical line of symmetry
   A = second curve is a rotation of the first
   R = second curve is a rotation of the first that has been reflected

9. **D CI**
   G = small black hexagon, D = small vertical-striped hexagon, C = small horizontal-striped hexagon
   K = large hexagon on the left of the figure, L = large hexagon is at the top of the figure, I = large hexagon is at the bottom of the figure

10. **A BN**
    L = large shape has five sides, B = large shape has six sides, P = large shape has four sides
    O = large shape has solid sides, T = large shape has bold sides, N = large shape has dashed sides

11. **B HG**
    H = lower two shapes are a parallelogram above a triangle
    J = lower two shapes are a triangle above a parallelogram
    K = upper two shapes are a triangle above a trapezium
    C = upper two shapes are a trapezium above a triangle
    G = upper two shapes are an oval above a triangle

12. **E AZ**
    Y = lower shape is a rounded rectangle
    A = lower shape is a rhombus
    S = lower shape is a parallelogram
    R = upper shape is a cube
    Q = upper shape is a cylinder
    Z = upper shape is a cuboid
    F = upper shape is a pyramid

Section 2
E.g. C
P1. E
P2. A
1. D
2. B
3. A
4. C
5. C
6. E
7. B
8. C
9. A
10. D
11. E
12. B

Section 3
E.g. D
Both figures on the left have solid lines.

P1. B
Both figures on the left are isosceles triangles with a horizontal base and have a black shape enclosed within them.

P2. E
Both figures on the left have an odd number of sides.

1. **D**
   Both figures on the left have three straight sides and two curved sides – one convex and one concave.

2. **E**
   Both largest figures on the left have straight lines. The number of black triangles within the largest figure is one more than the number of circles overlapping it.

3. **B**
   Both figures on the left have six lines creating four enclosed spaces within the figure.

4. **E**
   Both figures on the left have a bold curved line outside a dashed curved line, with an arrow pointing towards the curved lines.

5. **A**
   Both figures on the left are made up of three lines. At the ends of the lines are two identical large shapes (which are not in consecutive positions), a black circle and a black rhombus.

6. **B**
   Both figures on the left have a large shape, with horizontal-striped shading, that has a bold lined circle overlapping it. There is a smaller triangle with vertical-striped shading. There is a quadrilateral with dashed sides.

7. **A**
   Both figures on the left have a large white shape and a black shape below it. The white shape has two more sides than the black.

8. **D**
   Both figures on the left have four dividing lines, none of them parallel with one another. Three of the dividing lines are the same style as one another, and the fourth is different style.

9. **A**
   Both figures on the left have a black figure on the front face of the cube, a white shape on the right-hand face of the cube, and a dotted quadrilateral on the top face of the cube.
10. **C**
    Both figures on the left have two overlapping shapes. The one with fewer sides has an arrow pointing anticlockwise around the shape, and the one with more sides has an arrow pointing clockwise around the shape.
11. **C**
    Both figures on the left have a large rhombus with a black shape inside. The black shape has the same number of sides as the regular polygon that overlaps the large rhombus. Inside the rhombus there is a shape with vertical-striped shading, which is matched by an unshaded shape of the same size that overlaps the side of the rhombus.
12. **E**
    Both figures on the left have (moving clockwise around the figure) a circle, an arrow with a curved arrowhead, an arrow with a straight arrowhead, and a dashed triangle.

Section 4
E.g. A
P1. A
P2. D
1. C
2. E
3. B
4. E
5. B
6. A
7. B
8. E
9. D
10. A
11. B
12. C

Section 5
E.g. C
All of the figures across the bottom are black triangles. All of the figures across the top are black squares.

P1. **B**
All of the figures across the top are fine-pointed stars. All of the figures across the bottom are circles with an overlapping, thicker-pointed star.

P2. **B**
All of the figures across the top are arrowheads pointing towards a curved-cornered square. All of the figures across the bottom are rhombuses above a black, curved-cornered square. Flowing across all triangles is a dashed horizontal line.

1. **D**
Moving from left to right across the grid, the number of sides in the regular polygon decreases from eight to five, before starting again with eight sides. All of the figures across the top triangles have open arrowheads and all of the figures across the bottom have closed, black, triangular arrowheads.

2. **D**
Moving from left to right across the grid, across the bottom the black-and-white rectangle reflects from one figure to the next. Across the top, the black-and-white arrow and black triangle reflect from one figure to the next.

3. **B**
Moving from left to right across the grid, across the bottom the first two figures are translated into the third figure. Across the top, the first two figures are translated into the third figure. At the top and bottom, the number of points in the star gives the number of sides on the polygon in the third figure. The second figure gives the endpoints for the radiating lines in the third figure.

4. **A**
Moving from left to right across the grid, the divided square rotates 90 degrees anticlockwise in each figure.

5. **A**
Moving from left to right across the grid, each circle moves one position upwards.

6. **B**
Moving from left to right across the grid, the black triangle rotates 90 degrees anticlockwise in each figure. The pentagon alternates between black and white shading. The striped circle rotates 45 degrees anticlockwise. The striped rhombus does not change. The small shapes are arranged in different positions in each figure.

7. **C**
The figures come in pairs of one bottom figure and one top figure. Moving left to right across the grid, the second shape in the bottom figure is turned into the outer shape in the top figure. The first shape in the bottom figure changes to become the second-largest shape in the top figure. The third shape in the bottom figure changes colour and becomes the second-smallest shape in the top figure. The fourth shape in the bottom figure changes to become the smallest shape in the top figure.

8. **D**
Each of the figures across the bottom has a vertical line. Along the vertical line, there are two other lines – one bold and one with a black arrowhead. In the figures across the bottom, the arrow appears in three separate places – at the middle, bottom, then top of the vertical line. This is the same across the top, in the same order. In the figures across the bottom, there is a short, bold line that appears at the bottom, top, then middle of the vertical line. This is the same for the solid, short line across the top, in the same order.

9. **E**
In the figures across the bottom, the number of sides increases by one each time. The figures across the bottom all have dotted shading. The figures across the top all have white shading and the number of sides increases by one each time.

10. **B**
Across the bottom, the same four figures appear, and across the top the same four figures appear. Moving from left to right across the grid, the small figures are moved as follows: bottom left figure moves to bottom right; bottom right figure moves to top right; top right figure moves to bottom left; top left figure does not move. The figures then move back to their original positions for the third triangle in the sequence across the top and across the bottom.

11. **A**
Moving from left to right across the grid, the main part of the figures across the bottom is identical and the main part of the figures across the top is identical. Across the top and bottom, an open arrow is added in the second figure and this open arrow remains in the same position in the third figure. In the third figure, a black-shaded arrow is added.

12. **D**
Moving from left to right across the grid, the arrows alternate between clockwise and anticlockwise, and gain one additional loop.

Practice Test C Answers and Explanations

Section 1
E.g. A
Moving from left to right, the figure has been reflected in a horizontal mirror line.
P1. C
Moving from left to right, the overlapping figures are changed to simply an outline.
P2. E
Moving from left to right, the two figures swap position and size, but the shading of each figure does not change.
1. D
Moving from left to right, the white-shaded figure is subtracted from the black-shaded figure.
2. D
Moving from left to right, the shading moves one place upwards.
3. E
Moving from left to right, the figure is reflected in a vertical mirror line, the black-shaded shapes change to white, and the dotted lines change to dashed.
4. D
Moving from left to right, the figure is reflected in a vertical mirror line, the star gains one additional point, and the white-filled shape gains horizontal-striped shading.
5. A
Moving from left to right, the black shading does not move. The dotted shading changes to vertical stripes, and the white and diagonal-striped shading swap places.
6. D
Moving from left to right, the large rectangle is reflected in a vertical mirror line, and the black-shaded figure at the top of the rectangle is duplicated in the top right and bottom left corners.
7. E
Moving from left to right, the figure is changed to only an outline and is then reflected in a horizontal mirror line.
8. C
Moving from left to right, the inner figures gain one additional side, are overlapped and rotated 90 degrees clockwise. The figure on the right-hand side is placed the front of the others.
9. E
Moving from left to right, the number of scallops is changed to the number of concentric circles. The single rectangle underneath the scallops moves under the concentric circles.
10. D
Moving from left to right, the figure is reflected in a vertical mirror line.
11. C
Moving from left to right, there is a large shape and five smaller shapes overlapping. The two smaller white shapes are rotated 180 degrees, and the bottom, right-hand, black-shaded shape changes to white. The left-hand, small, black-shaded shape gains dotted shading. The top black-shaded, small shape gains diagonal-striped shading.
12. E
Moving from left to right, the largest shape changes to a dashed outer line and is rotated 180 degrees. The small fine shape within it changes to bold and is placed at the bottom of the figure. The bold small shape is changed to fine-lined and placed above the new bold figure.

Section 2
E.g. D
All of the figures have solid lines except for option D, which has dashed lines.
P1. E
All of the figures have pointed corners except for option E, which has curved corners.
P2. B
All of the other triangles have a right angle.
1. B
All of the figures are a rotation of one another except for B, which is a reflection.
2. D
All of the other figures have 12 sides in total.
3. B
All of the other figures contain a large irregular polygon with seven sides as the largest shape in the figure.
4. D
All of the other figures have the hexagon overlapping on the right-hand side.
5. D
In all of the other figures, if the polygons each have an odd number of sides, the black polygon is positioned at the top of the larger one. If the polygons each have an even number of sides, the black polygon is positioned at the bottom of the larger one.
6. E
In all of the other figures, the small shapes inside the circle and square are rotated 180 degrees from each other.
7. C
In all of the other figures, there is a circle at the bottom right-hand corner of each triangle.
8. B
In all of the other figures, the circles are arranged to create at least two lines of symmetry.
9. D
In all of the other figures, the black circle is at the end of a point on the star.
10. A
In all of the other figures, the two overlapping shapes at the top are identical to one another.
11. B
In all of the other figures, starting with the semicircle, the three shapes overlapping the circle are (in a clockwise direction) semicircle, oval and sector.
12. C
All of the figures are rotations of one another except for C, which is a reflection.

Section 3
E.g. B
P1. D
P2. C
1. E
2. B
3. A
4. E
5. C
6. A
7. D
8. E
9. A
10. D
11. B
12. A

Section 4
E.g. C

P1. A

P2. E

1. B
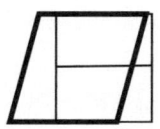

2. A

3. A
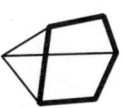

4. E
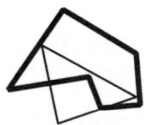

5. C

6. B

7. C

8. D
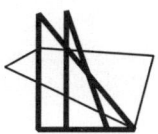

9. E
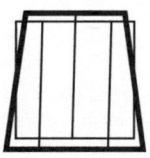

10. A

11. E

12. E

Section 5
E.g. A
P1. C
P2. E
1. B
2. D
3. D
4. A
5. E
6. B
7. E
8. E
9. B
10. B
11. A
12. E

Practice Test D Answers and Explanations

Section 1

E.g. E
From the left, a larger square is added as the series progresses. The outer square is always shaded dark grey.

P1. D
From the left, the shading moves clockwise around the shape. The diamond features a line fill in the pattern: dashed, thin, thick, dashed, thin.

P2. C
From the left, the shape rotates 90 degrees anticlockwise. The line style alternates between a dotted and solid line. One circle is added in each step of the series from the bottom of the shape.

1. D
From the left, the whole figure rotates 90 degrees clockwise. The shading in the circle alternates between the outer and inner sections. An extra peak is added to the line as the series progresses.

2. C
From the left, the shape rotates 90 degrees clockwise. The shading is in the pattern: grey, line fill, white, grey, line fill. The circle alternates between each side of the shape, starting furthest away from the black triangle, then moving next to it.

3. E
From the left, the shaded segment increases in size as the series progresses. The bottom left corner alternates between a cross and a plus with the line style pattern: thick, thin, dashed, thick, thin.

4. B
From the left, the 'V' moves up as the series progresses and the circle moves down and across. The triangle on the left-hand side alternates and the shape on the right-hand side alternates between a square and a triangle.

5. A
From the left, the outer line rotates 90 degrees anticlockwise. The inner line rotates 90 degrees clockwise. The outer line style goes in the pattern: dashed, thin, thick, dashed, thin. The inner line style goes in the pattern: thick, dashed, thin, thick, dashed.

6. C
From the left, the black shading moves around the figure anticlockwise. The double line segment moves clockwise around the figure. The number of sides of the interior figure increases by one as the series progresses.

7. B
From the left, the whole figure rotates 90 degrees anticlockwise and an additional line is added to the corner each time.

8. E
The shape flips in a vertical mirror line, and the shading in the square alternates between inside and outside the circle. From the left, the line fill in the large segment of the shape goes in the pattern: vertical, horizontal, diagonal, vertical, horizontal.

9. C
From the left, the shape's number of sides increases by one. The shape's line fill style goes in the pattern: vertical, horizontal, crossed, vertical, horizontal.

10. D
The large shape flips in a vertical mirror line. The arrow flips in a horizontal mirror line. From the left, the number of circles goes in the pattern: one, two, three, one, two.

11. C
From the left, the shape alternates and rotates 90 degrees clockwise. The shading moves anticlockwise around the shape.

12. D
From the left, the parallelogram moves down through the series until the third figure then moves upwards. The ellipse moves up through the series until the third figure, then moves down. The parallelogram's line style goes in the pattern: thin, dashed, thick, thin, dashed.

Section 2

E.g. B
A quarter of the shape is shaded dark grey.

P1. D
The figure features three identical shapes of any size and orientation.

P2. C
There is a shaded triangle inside a larger shape. Two of the sides of the triangle are within the larger shape.

1. C
The shapes have six sides.

2. D
The figure features two identical shapes, one smaller than the other.

3. A
There are three shapes, one of which is a rounded shape. The rounded shape is always shaded.

4. E
Five lines make up the long line and three arrowheads face the same direction along the line.

5. C
The shape is divided into four equal parts.

6. B
There are two overlapping shapes; one shape is always a triangle. The shapes are shaded where they overlap.

7. E
The lines at every corner extend beyond the corner.

8. C
The figures feature one line of horizontal symmetry and no vertical symmetry.

9. B
The figures feature a seven-sided shape with three circles overlapping the sides. The position of the circles and the position of their shade are distractors.

10. E
There are four identical shapes in each figure all connected at at least one point. The number of shapes shaded and the position is a distractor.

11. D
The figure is made up of a shape and a line and features one line of vertical symmetry.

12. C
Within the larger shape is a five-sided shape that shares one side only with the larger shape. The position of the shading is a distractor.

Section 3

E.g. B GLP
F, G = large shape
F = triangle; G = circle

K, L = shade
K = grey; L = no shade

P, Q = small shape
P = circle; Q = square

P1. C QGW
P, Q = large shape
P = hexagon; Q = bow tie

F, G = left-hand side fill
F = vertical lines; G = horizontal lines

W, X, Y = right-hand side fill
W = white; X = grey; Y = black

P2. **A KRY**
   K, L, M = large shape
   K = parallelogram; L = trapezium; M = rectangle

   P, Q, R = line style
   P = dashed; Q = thin; R = thick

   W, X, Y, Z = number of circles
   W = two; X = three; Y = one; Z = four

1. **C GLP**
   F, G = shade of shape on the right
   F = black; G = white

   K, L = number of sections the rectangle is divided into
   K = four; L = two

   P, Q = rectangle line style
   P = thick; Q = thin

2. **B QKY**
   P, Q = position of line
   P = above the square; Q = below the square

   K, L = square fill
   K = cross; L = plus

   W, X, Y = line style
   W = thin; X = thick; Y = dashed

3. **E HPL**
   F, G, H = circle size
   F = medium; G = large; H = small

   P, Q = proportion of circle shaded
   P = quarter; Q = half

   K, L = shade
   K = grey; L = black

4. **A FLZ**
   F, G = large shape
   F = square with top left corner missing; G = square with top right corner missing

   K, L = corner triangle shade
   K = grey; L = white

   X, Y, Z = line pattern inside the shape
   X = plus; Y = cross; Z = diagonal lines

5. **C QLW**
   P, Q = orientation of line
   P = line in 'm' orientation; Q = line in 'w' orientation

   K, L = position of circle in relation to line
   K = circle outside of the line; L = circle inside of the line

   W, X, Y = right-hand side shape
   W = rectangle; X = ellipse; Y = bow tie

   Distractor = line style

6. **B GLW**
   F, G = number of sides of shape
   F = five; G = six

   K, L = circle shade
   K = black; L = white

   W, X, Y = shade
   W = grey; X = white; Y = black

7. **E MQZ**
   K = upright 'U' shape; L = 'U' shape rotated 90 degrees anticlockwise; M = 'U' shape rotated 180 degrees

   P, Q, R = position of interior line
   P = line through the centre of the shape; Q = line through the right-hand side of the shape; R = line through the left-hand side of the shape

   W, X, Y, Z = small shape
   W = square; X = circle; Y = triangle; Z = rectangle

8. **D FMQ**
   F, G, H = shape at the bottom of the figure
   F = thick part of the shape on the left-hand side; G = 'T' shape; H = thick part of the shape on the right-hand side

   K, L, M = top two lines
   K = dashed and thick line; L = thick and thin line; M = dotted and thin line

   P, Q, R, S = number of sections the bottom shape is divided into
   P = four; Q = two; R = three; S = one

9. **C LRX**
   K, L, M = orientation of triangle
   K = long edge vertical, short edge horizontal to the left-hand side; L = long edge horizontal, short edge vertical towards the base of the figure; M = long edge horizontal, short edge vertical towards the top of the figure

   P, Q, R, S = number of circles shaded
   P = three; Q = four; R = two; S = one

   X, Y, Z = triangle fill
   X = lines parallel to the long edge of the triangle; Y = lines parallel to the short edge of the triangle; Z = lines parallel to the diagonal line of the triangle

10. **B HPY**
    F, G, H = orientation of the pentagon
    F = pointing upwards; G = pointing downwards, 180-degree rotation of the first figure; H = pointing towards the right, 90-degree clockwise rotation of the first figure

    P, Q, R = number of sides of small shape inside
    P = five; Q = three; R = four

    W, X, Y, Z = fill type
    W = white; X = grey; Y = black; Z = dotted

11. **A LPZ**
    K, L, M = number of sides of the shape
    K = six; L = eight; M = seven

    P, Q, R = line style of the shape
    P = thin; Q = dashed; R = thick

    W, X, Y, Z = number of outer line segments
    W = two; X = five; Y = four; Z = three

12. **E MQW**
    K, L, M = configuration of shapes
    K = line, thin rectangle, thick rectangle; L = thin rectangle, line, thick rectangle; M = thin rectangle, thick rectangle, line

    P, Q, R = thin rectangle fill
    P = vertical lines; Q = diagonal lines; R = cross

    W, X, Y, Z = thick rectangle fill
    W = cross; X = vertical lines; Y = horizontal lines; Z = diagonal lines

    Distractor = line style

Section 4

E.g. B
Each row has the same shape. Each column has the same fill style.

P1. D
The arrow shape rotates clockwise in each row from the left. The line style in each row is the same. Each row features an ellipse with grey, white and black fill in a different order.

P2. C
The large shape in each row is the same. The whole figure rotates anticlockwise moving across the row from the left. Each column has the same fill style. Each row features a triangle shaded black, grey and white in a different order.

1. C
Each row features the same shape which moves down through the square from the left. Every shape is divided into three sections. In each row every section is shaded in a different order.

2. B
From the left, the outer line rotates 90 degrees clockwise in rows. The square rotates 90 degrees anticlockwise in rows.

3. E
Each column features the same shape which rotates clockwise moving down. Each row features the same line style.

4. B
Each column features the same shape which gets smaller moving down. The shading in the shape alternates between the top and bottom of the shape. Moving down, a line is added to the figure with each row. The bottom line in each column has the same line style.

5. D
Each row features the same three shapes in a different order. The shapes in each row are divided in the same way. Half of the shape has the same fill style in columns.

6. C
Each row features the same shape which rotates 90 degrees anticlockwise moving left to right. The shape has a thick, dashed and dotted line style in a different order for every row. From the left, the circle moves clockwise around the large shape in rows.

7. E
Each row features the same shape which moves upwards in the square moving left to right. In rows, the shape is always overlapped by one, two or three lines in a different order. From the left, the styles of the three lines are always in the order: thin, dashed, thick.

8. B
Each row features three shapes in a different order. The shaded segment moves clockwise around the shapes down each column.

9. D
Each row features the same figure which rotates 90 degrees clockwise moving left to right. Each column has the same line style. Shading moves across the shape along each row.

10. C
The whole figure rotates 90 degrees clockwise in rows left to right. Triangles in each row are shaded white, grey and black in a different order. Circles in each row feature grey, cross and white fill in a different order.

11. B
The whole figure rotates 90 degrees clockwise in rows left to right. The line style of the large rectangle is the same in columns. The medium-sized rectangle has the same fill in rows. The squares have a cross, plus and vertical line fill in a different order for each row.

12. C
The whole figure rotates 90 degrees clockwise in rows left to right. The shading alternates from left to right in rows. A dashed, thin and dotted line features in a different order for each row.

Section 5

E.g. C
P1. B
P2. D
1. A
2. D
3. A
4. C
5. B
6. D
7. D
8. C
9. E
10. B
11. E
12. B

NON-VERBAL REASONING TEST A

NVR A

Pupil's Name

School Name

Date of Test

PUPIL NUMBER
SCHOOL NUMBER
DATE OF BIRTH

Day	Month		Year	
[0] [0]	January	☐	2011	☐
[1] [1]	February	☐	2012	☐
[2] [2]	March	☐	2013	☐
[3] [3]	April	☐	2014	☐
[4]	May	☐	2015	☐
[5]	June	☐	2016	☐
[6]	July	☐	2017	☐
[7]	August	☐	2018	☐
[8]	September	☐	2019	☐
[9]	October	☐	2020	☐
	November	☐	2021	☐
	December	☐	2022	☐

Please mark like this ⊢.

SECTION 1

SECTION 2

© HarperCollins*Publishers*

NVR A

PUPIL NUMBER

SECTION 3

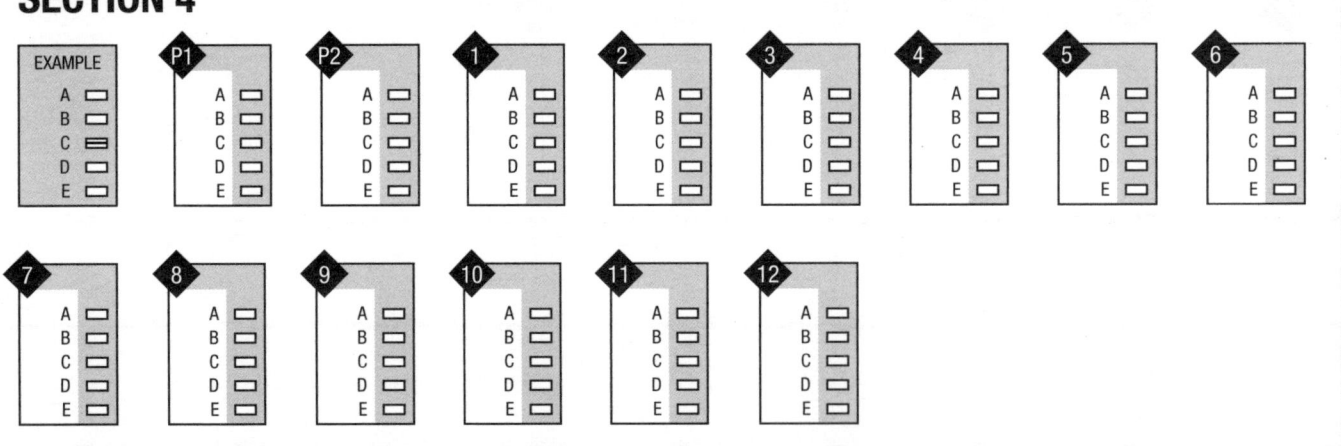

SECTION 4

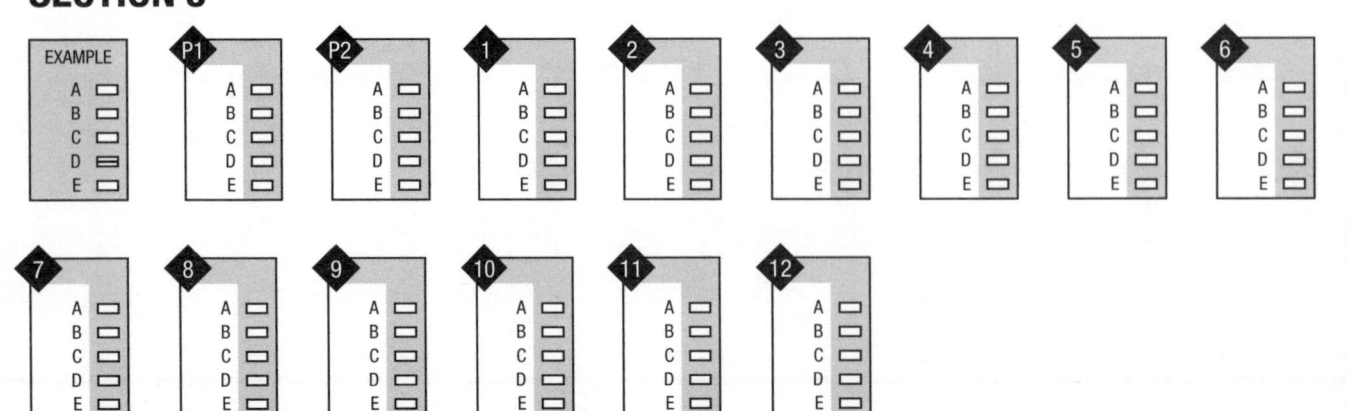

SECTION 5

NON-VERBAL REASONING TEST B

Pupil's Name

School Name

Date of Test

SECTION 1

SECTION 2

NVR B

PUPIL NUMBER

SECTION 3

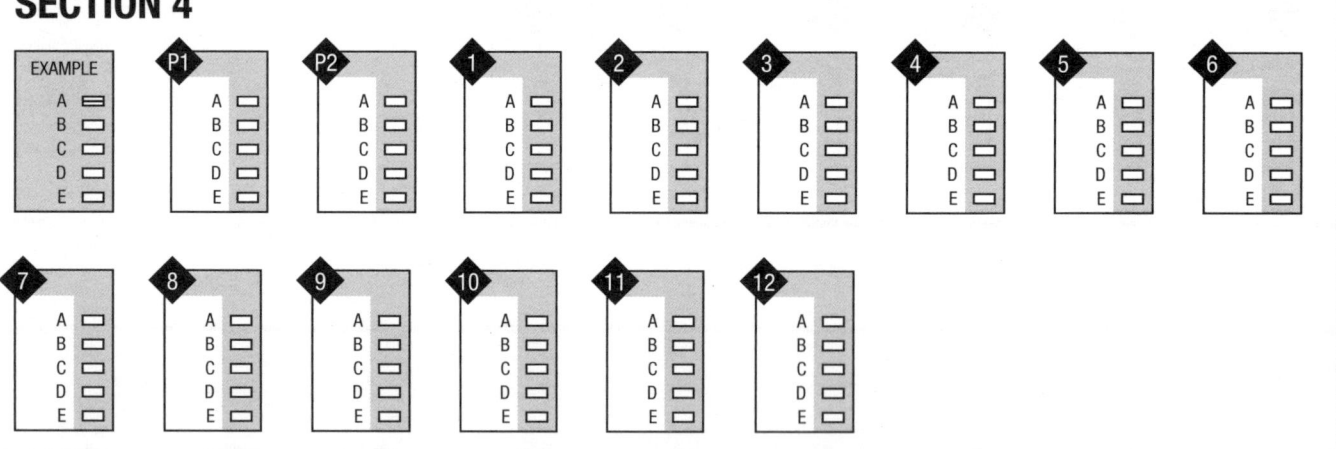

SECTION 4

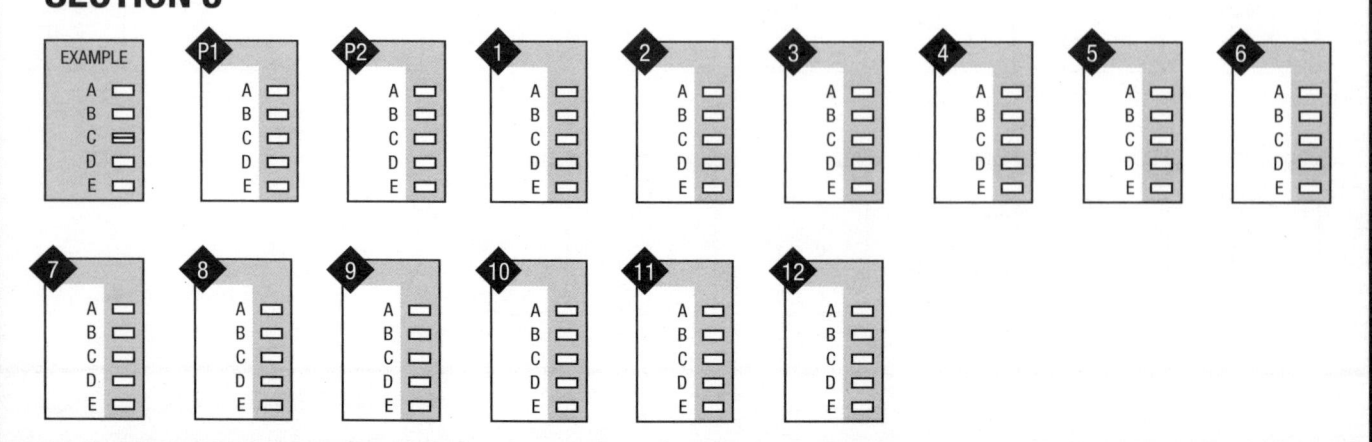

SECTION 5

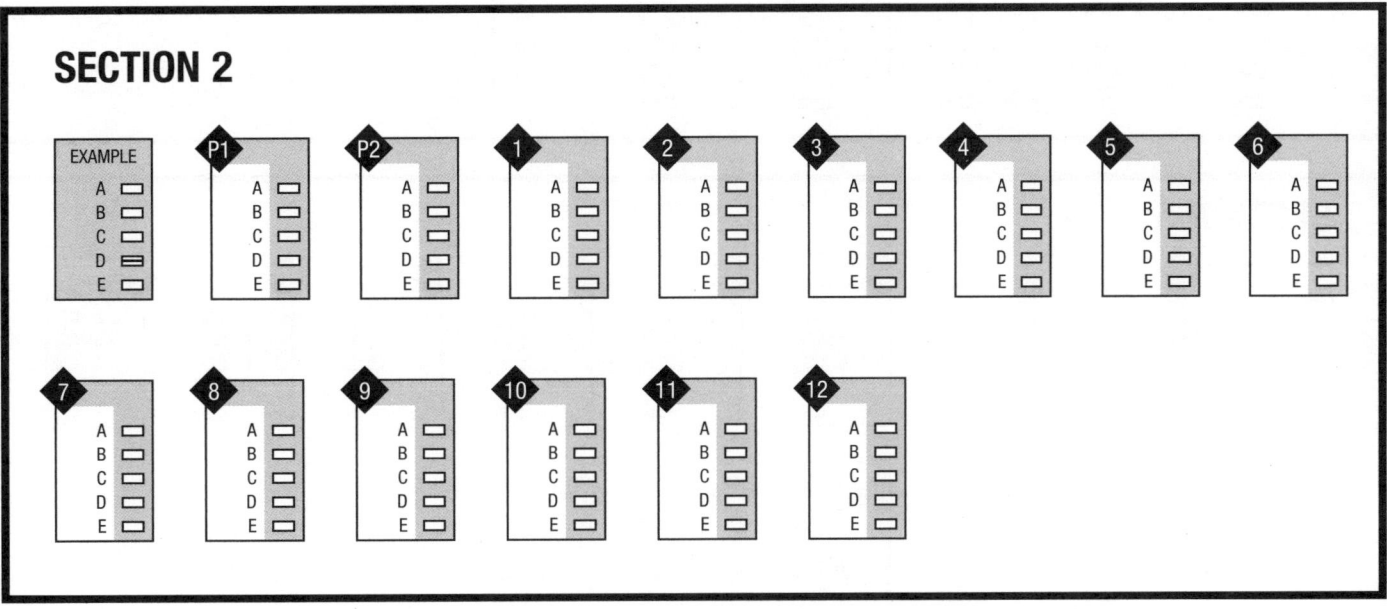

SECTION 3

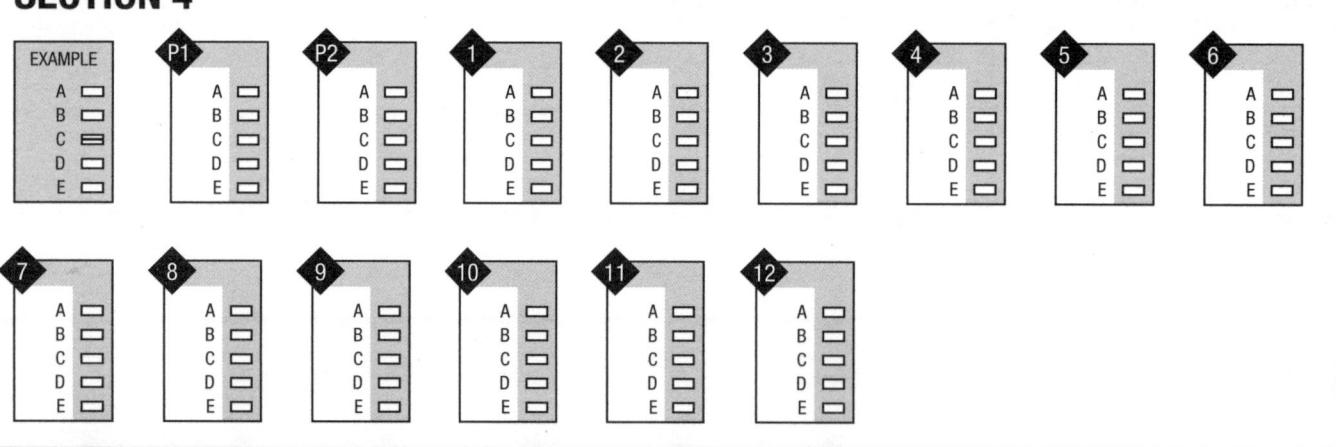

SECTION 4

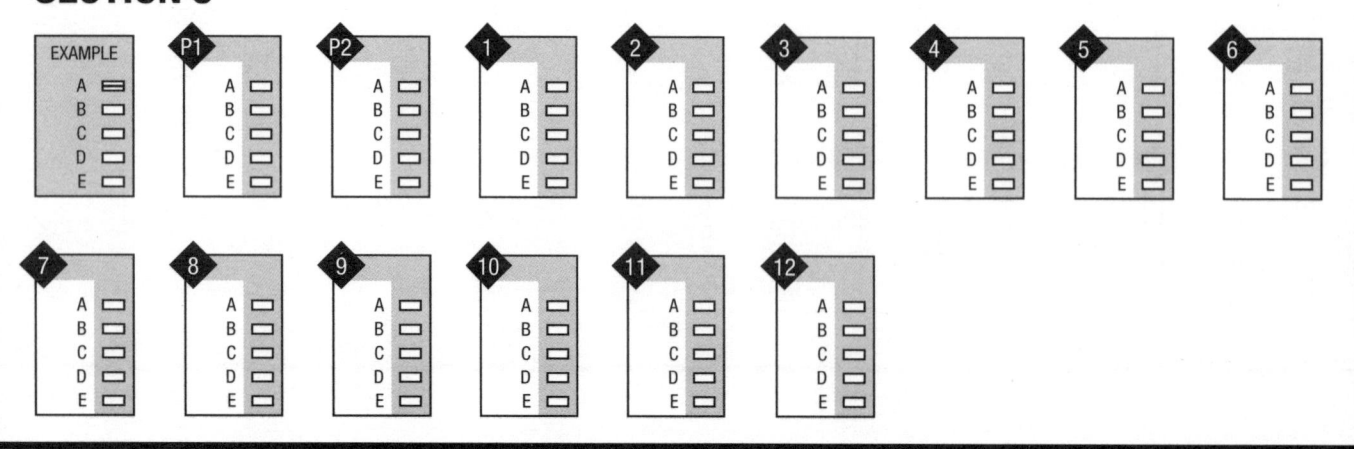

SECTION 5

NON-VERBAL REASONING TEST D

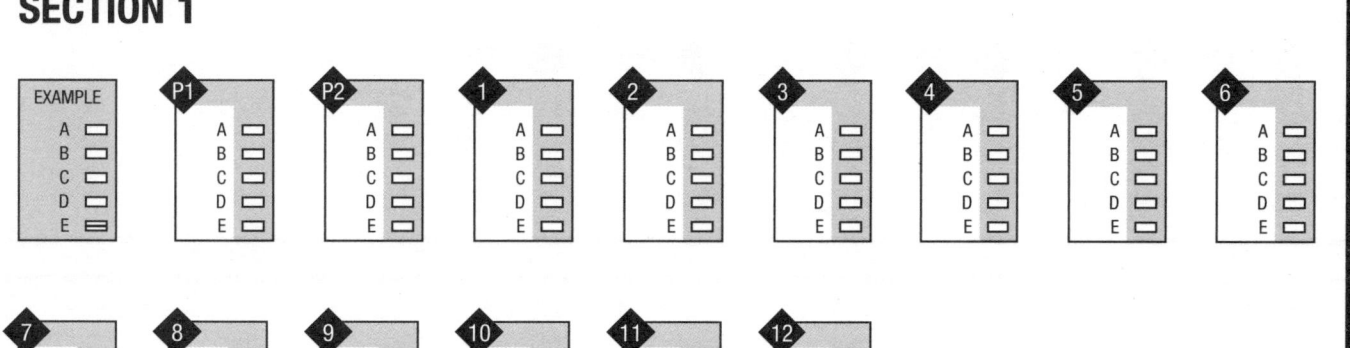

SECTION 1

SECTION 2

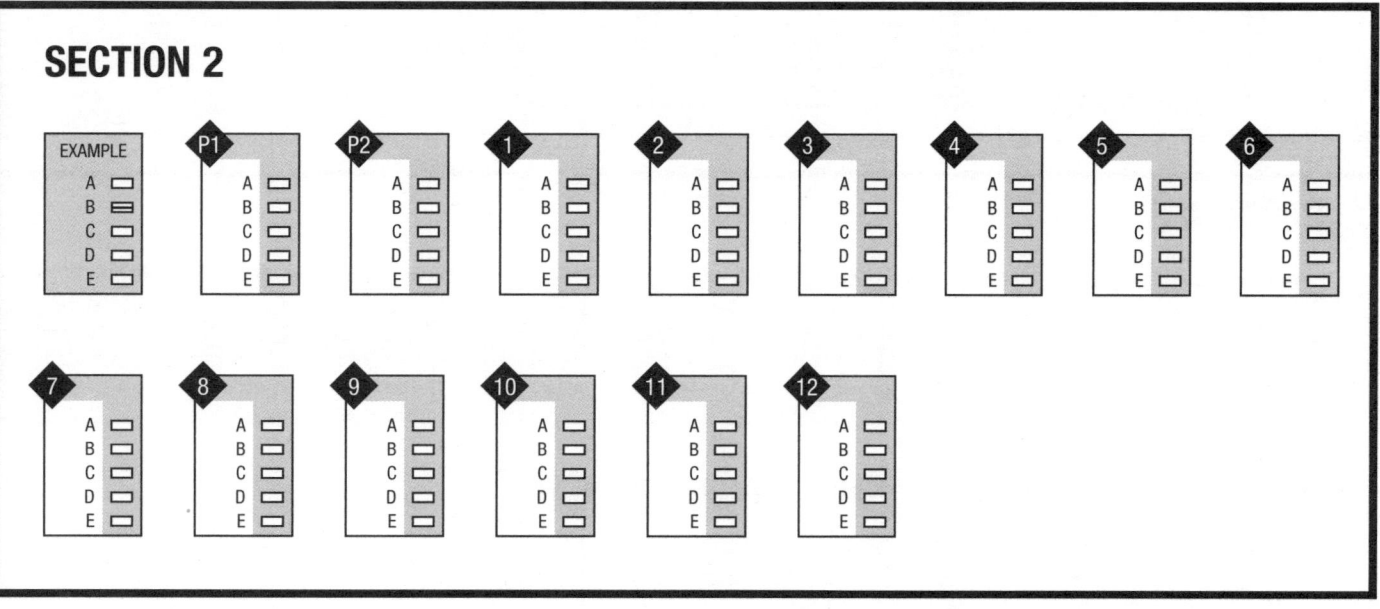

© HarperCollins*Publishers*

NVR D

PUPIL NUMBER

SECTION 3

SECTION 4

SECTION 5